Da

THE UNWRITTEN PHILOSOPHY
AND OTHER ESSAYS

THE
UNWRITTEN PHILOSOPHY
AND OTHER ESSAYS

BY

F. M. CORNFORD

*Late Laurence Professor of Ancient Philosophy
and Fellow of Trinity College in the
University of Cambridge*

EDITED WITH AN
INTRODUCTORY MEMOIR
BY

W. K. C. GUTHRIE

CAMBRIDGE
AT THE UNIVERSITY PRESS
1967

PUBLISHED BY
THE SYNDICS OF THE CAMBRIDGE UNIVERSITY PRESS

Bentley House, 200 Euston Road, London, N.W.1
American Branch: 32 East 57th Street, New York, N.Y. 10022

88601

First Published 1950
Reprinted 1967
First paperback edition 1967

First printed in Great Britain at the University Press, Cambridge
Reprinted, by Lithography, in Great Britain by
Hazell Watson & Viney Ltd,
Aylesbury, Bucks

CONTENTS

v

MEMOIR

CORNFORD once began a paragraph with the words: 'As I am neither a philosopher nor a theologian....' What then was he? The best answer I can give is that he was a historian and a poet, and in his chosen field, the history of Greek thought, a better historian because he was a poet. The cosmology of the Pythagoreans, though in due course to be explained in terms of mathematical philosophy, brings first of all to his mind the picture of Lorenzo and Jessica lying on the moonlit grass. It recalls

> There's not the smallest orb which thou behold'st
> But in his motion like an angel sings,
> Still quiring to the young-eyed cherubins;
> Such harmony is in immortal souls.

This approach is not merely pleasanter, but truer. As he himself said when describing the advantage of expressing one's thoughts, as Plato did, in dramatic form: 'the action is lifted above the plane of historical fact towards the region of poetry and universal statement, which Aristotle describes as "more philosophic and of graver import" than the particular statements of history'. A philosopher, and even a historian of recent European philosophy, need not, perhaps, be a poet. But the sympathetic insight of a naturally poetic mind was exactly what was needed for the task which he had set himself of exploring the foundations of ancient thought. 'Plato was born into a society where the means of expression were grotesquely inadequate to the demands of abstract speculation. Philosophic prose was in its lisping infancy. The fifth century had been an age in which profound and far-reaching thoughts had been released to hover, as it were, in a disembodied state, and haunt the minds of men who could not capture more than a fragment of their meaning in the precision of a formula.' When he wrote these words he was not defending his own approach to the Greeks, but they go far in themselves to explain the necessity for the insight to which I have referred.

Again, speaking of Empedocles and the doctrine of the transmigration of souls, he wrote (in his last, unfinished work):

The unity of all life, the kinship of all living things, is the fundamental principle; and we cannot dismiss the notion that it is based on some genuine psychological experience, merely because we do not believe in transmigration and are not poets. Books on psychology have mostly been written by philosophers and men of science whose habits of thought are uncongenial to that poetic imagination (as we call it) which can 'see into the life of things' and lose the sense of separate existence in a communion of feeling with the whole of nature, as if the daughters of Memory could free the soul from the limitations of space as well as from those of time. It is not wise, or even genuinely scientific, to brush aside as idle fancy or outworn superstition the experience of the greatest poets, because it is beyond the reach of the ordinary man and cannot be translated into terms of what he would call an 'explanation'. The philosophy of Empedocles, whether we like it or not, is animated and illuminated from within by this poetic and prophetic gift of insight, though, here as elsewhere, the Muses may sometimes be telling a false tale that is only like the truth.

In his later years he said that it sometimes seemed to him as if he had been all his life writing one and the same book. For all the difference between *Thucydides Mythistoricus* at one end and *Plato and Parmenides* at the other, it is true that one guiding thought can be followed throughout the whole remarkable series, one paramount lesson which he was always trying to bring home to our duller minds. This comprised, first, a basic truth about the nature of human thought, and secondly, its application to the Greeks. In his inaugural lecture of 1931, the general truth is enunciated thus:

If we look beneath the surface of philosophical discussion, we find that its course is largely governed by assumptions that are seldom, or never, mentioned. I mean that groundwork of current conceptions shared by all the men of any given culture and never mentioned because it is taken for granted as obvious.

He supports it by a quotation from A. N. Whitehead: 'When you are criticizing the philosophy of an epoch, do not chiefly direct your attention to those intellectual positions which its exponents feel it necessary explicitly to defend. There will be some fundamental assumptions which adherents of all the variant systems within the epoch unconsciously presuppose.'[1] But in the preface to his first book, published in 1907, we can already read: 'In every age the common interpretation of the world of things is controlled by some scheme of unchallenged and unsuspected presupposition; and the mind of any individual, however little he may think himself to be in sympathy with his contemporaries, is not an insulated compartment, but more like a pool in one continuous medium—the circumambient atmosphere of his place and time. This element of thought is always, of course, most difficult to detect and analyse, just because it is a constant factor which underlies all the differential characters of many minds.'[2]

The particular application of this lesson, that is, the answer to the question what is the groundwork of current conceptions, what are the unmentioned because unconscious presuppositions in the special case of the Greeks, cannot well be set forth here. It can only be found by following Cornford as he finds it himself in Thucydides, in the philosophers, in the tragic or comic poets, and each must decide as he reads how far the answer is justified. We may, however, attempt a brief indication of it. Greek philosophical and historical writing, however rational and scientific in intention, and whatever the mental powers of its authors, was the work of men born into an entirely different climate of thought from their modern counterparts. It lacked not only a background of systematically accumulated knowledge, but also the framework of scientific concepts and categories within which that background has since been built up. To-day both are the common heritage of even the less highly educated and the less gifted of us, a heritage from which the most independent minds would find it hard, even if they wished, to shake themselves free. Yet 'the philosophic Muse is not a motherless Athena'. Lacking our complex apparatus of experimentally ascertained fact and laboriously constructed

[1] A. N. Whitehead, *Science and the Modern World* (1925), p. 71. Cf. p. 39 below.
[2] *Thucydides Mythistoricus* (1907), p. ix.

(though now almost unconsciously applied) logic, her image was inevitably cast in another mould. 'If the individual intellect is her father, her older and more august parent is religion.' 'Religion expresses itself in poetical symbols and in terms of mythical personalities. Philosophy prefers the language of dry abstraction, and speaks of *substance, cause, matter*, and so forth. But the outward difference only disguises an inward and substantial affinity between these two successive products of the same consciousness. The modes of thought that attain to clear definition and explicit statement in philosophy were already implicit in the unreasoned intuitions of mythology.'[1]

This approach to the philosophers is obviously in large measure psychological, and we can understand the deep interest awakened in Cornford's mind by the Zürich school of psychologists when we read in the works of Jung that 'philosophy is internally nothing else but a refined and sublimated mythology'. Such confirmation from another quarter must have seemed striking. In his own progress towards the same conclusion he had been helped, not by the analogies of psycho-analysis but rather by theories of the earliest types of social organisation and the mentality which resulted from them, by accounts of the 'group-soul' and 'collective representations' as they were emerging from the researches of French scholars, notably Emil Durkheim and Levy-Bruhl. The 'collective unconscious' of Jung came later to strengthen and deepen his convictions.

This view of the progress of Greek thought was already in his mind when he wrote *Thucydides Mythistoricus*, a masterpiece of lucid and persuasive argument, in the preface to which we read: 'The history of philosophy is written as if Thales had suddenly dropped from the sky, and as he bumped the earth, ejaculated, "Everything must be made of water!"'[2] But it is first dealt with

---

[1] *From Religion to Philosophy* (1912), pp. ix, vii.

[2] *Thuc. Myth.* p. x. It is obvious from what has been said that Cornford's approach to ancient thought corresponded in important respects to the conception of history held by the late R. G. Collingwood. Thus too we find Cornford criticising (in an unpublished chapter) 'the assumption that the *questions they asked themselves*, the motives which prompted their inquiries, and the quarters to which they looked for the sources of knowledge, were the same

fully, as the title implies, in *From Religion to Philosophy*, which appeared in 1912. For one who only knew Cornford later, and was unaffected by the sources, both personal and literary, of his inspiration at that time, it is perhaps not easy to give a just appreciation of this work. Yet it is fair to say that it represents a necessary stage on the way to that comprehensive understanding of the Greek mind which he afterwards achieved, rather than an example of the full understanding itself. Its argument is that the Milesian philosophers, in stripping off the mythological and theological trappings from their account of the universe, whereby they believed themselves to be getting at the natural facts and offering purely rational explanations, were in fact going behind the religious phase and unconsciously reproducing a pre-religious type of thought which had all the time persisted underneath. Their conception of nature is not one which could have arisen from scientific observation, nor yet (since it has parallels not only in Indian philosophy but in primitive thinking wherever this has been laid bare by anthropologists) from the imagination of a single inspired individual. It is then traced, largely in reliance on the French school of sociologists mentioned above, to an origin in the state of mind of a totemic society which included not only men, but animals and trees, the sky, the earth and the whole universe within the same tribal divisions and allotted to them certain provinces as their own.

This theory leaves one now with a certain feeling of inadequacy. It belongs to the days when researchers still spoke of the 'origin' of religion, as if it could be assumed that this origin was single and moreover could be elicited without undue difficulty by observation and questioning of existing savage tribes. Thus Cornford writes: 'If we are right about the starting-point, we have both ends of the chain in our hands'. In reconstructing the intermediate links, i.e. the growth of Greek polytheistic religion up to the time when the Milesian philosophers rejected it, he emphasises the hypothetical nature of the account and the impossibility of its

then as now'. Compare Collingwood's 'logic of question and answer'. Collingwood's own comment on *Thucydides Mythistoricus* is brief and unqualified: 'He was of course perfectly right' (*The Idea of History*, p. 18).

being certain or complete. This is of course right, at least as far as the earlier stages are concerned, but surely the starting-point, namely that 'what the Milesians called *physis* has the same origin as what the savage calls *Mana*', is at least equally hypothetical. It is when he gets beyond this remote and misty starting-point and begins to demonstrate the different types of philosophy which are the natural successors of Olympian and mystery-religions respectively, and to reveal the links which unite the Milesians to the one and the Pythagoreans to the other—links which do not have to be inferred, but are there in extant Greek literature for him who has Cornford's eyes to see—that to some at least he will appear to be on ground that is both more solid in itself and more fruitful in explanation of the birth and early growth of the philosophic and scientific spirit in Europe.[1]

Cornford himself pays glowing tribute to the influence in these formative years of two minds with which he was in personal contact, those of A. W. Verrall and Jane Harrison. Verrall's lectures were imparting, with all the thrill and freshness of discovery, a way of interpreting the great classics of ancient literature as one would a work of modern poetry or prose; not reading back our own ideas into the ancient mind—far from it—but boldly

[1] In saying that the argument of *From Religion to Philosophy* is not completely satisfying, I am in part at least expressing what I have learned from Cornford himself. In the book which he was writing when he died he returns to the same problems with a mind matured and enriched by a lifetime's study, and suggests a fresh solution of the problem of the rise of anthropomorphism and its evolution into philosophy which relies far less on *a priori* argument and more on historical evidence. In particular he has assimilated and turned to his own purposes the findings of Prof. S. H. Hooke and his collaborators on the relationship between myth and ritual (in *Myth and Ritual*, 1933, and *The Labyrinth*, 1935), in which he saw the origin of much in Greek cosmogonical myth. Again, in arriving at a true estimate of the relation between the ostensibly rationalistic philosopher in Greece and his predecessors and contemporaries the seers, poets and rhapsodes, he felt further enlightened by the material collected by Mrs Chadwick (*Poetry and Prophecy*, 1942) on the composite character of the shaman and similar figures in northern Asia. For a connecting link between Greece and the mythology and ritual of Babylonia he now had the finds at Ras Shamra on the northern coast of Syria and the Canaanite mythology there revealed (Schaeffer, *The Cuneiform texts of Ras Shamra Ugarit*, 1939). Links with the northern shamans were already to hand in Orpheus, Zalmoxis and Hyperboreans like Aristeas and Abaris.

applying common sense and universal critical canons to the content · of a work, and daring to teach that the thought of an author was more important than his syntax. Of Cornford's friendship with Jane Harrison and all that it meant to him, one who did not know her can scarcely speak; but it would be difficult to overestimate the effect at this time of her infectious enthusiasm, her sympathetic understanding and her ready praise. The Cambridge school was still dominated by the tradition of strict linguistic scholarship and the minutiae of form. Brought up within these narrow walls, Cornford's heart went out to one who gloried that in her own time, as she has written in her reminiscences, classics were turning in their long sleep, that she had James Frazer for a contemporary, that she was a young graduate when Schliemann began to dig at Troy, and that when the relevance of these men to classical studies was beginning to force itself on the minds of scholars, 'Arthur Evans set sail for his new Atlantis and telegraphed news of the Minotaur from his own labyrinth'.[1] To the new and exciting influence of such thoughts as these he must have owed much of his appreciation of mythology as true history—the history of the mind of a people, which is only falsified and obscured if the myths are ignored or explained away.

Cornford's mind did not remain in tutelage. In what way did he go beyond these ideas and put them in their place as one element in the subtle complex of his later work? To answer the question is to attempt a statement of the essence of his achievement, and this, with due warning that one who is interested in the same subject-matter may be led to isolate the things which he himself wishes to find, I should like to do.

His unusual merit is his constant awareness that all systems of religious and philosophical thought have two sides, the conscious and the unconscious, or (to take another pair of rough equivalents) the intellectual and the instinctive. Greek minds were intellectually alive, inclined to logical and often mathematical activity, and delighted in building up elaborate structures of thought. Yet as we have noted, these structures were not created *in vacuo*, but based unconsciously on the innate preconceptions which centuries of

[1] *Reminiscences of a Student's Life* (1925), p. 83.

pre-intellectual mental processes had implanted. In his early account of the existence and nature of these preconceptions, Cornford was to a large extent inspired by the work of others—the French sociologists or Jane Harrison's researches into comparative mythology. What was his own was the historical sense and mental balance which enabled him, as he went on, to assign to each of the two sides its proper place and to give a just appreciation of the finished product of which each was only one ingredient. This evolutionary view of human thought came to him like a revelation, and to seize the primitive roots of Greek thought seemed to him essential to an understanding of its flower. It was an indispensable means to an end, but the end remained the same, to comprehend the mind of a Plato, an Aeschylus or a Thucydides. Here we may find the difference between him and some of those to whom in his early years he owed so much. Jane Harrison confessed, with the enthusiasm of a freedom won from a narrowly evangelical upbringing: 'I mention these ritual dances, this ritual drama, this bridge between art and life, because it is things like these that I was all my life blindly seeking.... Great things in literature, Greek plays for example, I most enjoy when behind their bright splendours I see moving darker and older shapes.' For her, clearly, in the study of Greek literature the primitive background was more than a means to an end. Set beside her words a sentence from a lecture which Cornford wrote twenty years or more after the publication of *From Religion to Philosophy*. After stating, in language of delicate parody, what he describes as 'an analytical account of Platonism', he continues: 'But such a description bears much the same relation to the processes in Plato's mind, as revealed in the dialogues, that an anatomical diagram bears to the breathing and moving man, who can live and love and work and die without any assistance from grotesque and hideous portraits of his internal economy.'

The focus of his interest was always the breathing and moving man. Such abstractions and hypothetical constructions as Primitive Man, Collective Representations or the Collective Psyche had an undeniable intrinsic interest, but they remained no more than useful instruments. To understand his instruments was the first task, and it is natural therefore that these conceptions loom more largely in his earlier books and that his own development seems in a way to have been a progress 'from religion to philosophy'.

His interest in Greek thought found expression in two particular fields, Presocratic philosophy and the mind of Plato. To those of us who were able to listen to his lectures on the Presocratics it is a matter of lasting regret that he died without completing a book entirely devoted to them. The lectures gave one the peculiar sensation of mental well-being which comes from following a skilfully and closely woven pattern of argument, of necessity intricate but never obscure. They had a perennial freshness, for he never tired of trying new approaches, suggested by his reading or his own thoughts, which might lead to a better solution of the problems involved, and himself so obviously enjoyed (for all the quiet dignity of his delivery) the opportunity for testing new ideas which the subject offered. At the risk of a short digression, it is worth mentioning his theory of the proper use of lectures, which are so often (and rightly) condemned as a mere repetition of what the student can get more conveniently, quickly and efficiently from books. In Cornford's view, ideas can and should be tried out in a lecture while they are in process of formation, before the scholar is ready to commit himself to them in print. Lectures should be a part of the humanist's laboratory, with the inestimable advantage to the listener that he is not presented with a finished treatise which he could better read in his own room, but is watching a living mind at work and given an insight into its methods. But Cornford's thoughts can never be expressed so well as in his own words. 'A course of lectures ought almost always to be the outcome of recent first-hand work. When a man's mind is full of fresh ideas and quickened by the excitement of discovery, then is the time to lecture, because then is the chance of interesting his class, while the discipline of exposition will test and clarify his results. The lectures over, the results should in many cases go at once into a book. Finally a period of rest, followed by fresh study of a different subject; and so the process begins again.'[1]

[1] *The Cambridge Classical Course* (1903), pp. 28 f.

He himself faithfully carried out his precept in the sequence of lectures and books on separate dialogues of Plato. If the lectures on the Presocratics did not result in a single book, the fruits of his meditations on them are to be found in many places in his writings. Something of the sureness of his historical sense in this field will, it is hoped, appear from one or two of the essays presented here. They should be supplemented by the chapter 'Mystery-Religions and Presocratic Philosophy' in the *Cambridge Ancient History*, vol. IV. The place of the Presocratics in the whole Greek philosophical tradition is admirably explained for the non-specialist in the lucid sketch called *Before and After Socrates*, itself the outcome of a course of extra-mural lectures.

In 1935 appeared the first of his books dealing with the later and more difficult dialogues of Plato. Two more were published, in 1937 and 1939. These works were the direct outcome of his lectures in the University, to which they owed their unique form. Their titles are *Plato's Theory of Knowledge*, *Plato's Cosmology* and *Plato and Parmenides*, with a sub-title to say that they consist of the *Theaetetus* and *Sophist*, or the *Timaeus* or the *Parmenides*, 'translated with a running commentary'. (The last mentioned also contains a translation of the fragments of Parmenides' own *Way of Truth*.) He had in fact retained exactly the method which he or any other lecturer would naturally use, of translating a paragraph and following it by his own explanation and comment before proceeding to the next. The reader is taken by the hand and guided through the argument like one of his own class, with illuminating results.

In these books he is dealing with the finished product, not the raw material or the first uncertain essays of Greek thought. The keen psychological and historical sense is always in evidence, but there is not the same need for the insight and inference by which the fragmentary hints of the earlier thinkers were taken up and their minds revealed against a background of yet older conceptions. With the complete dialogues before him, he had the opportunity for a more exact appreciation of the structure which the philosopher himself had built. His main effort was devoted to a patient and faithful dissection of the argument, in which his

historical imagination, and especially his keen awareness of the
historical associations of words, took him straight to the heart of
the reasoning and saved him time and again from entanglement
in merely verbal quibbles. Yet here too the amount of external
reading to be undertaken was considerable, if he was to succeed
in his constant aim of understanding his author by becoming
familiar with the intellectual climate in which he worked and the
influences to which his mind was open. His absorption in the
study of Plato's predecessors we already know. One other example may be mentioned, his serious and thorough reading in the
field of Greek mathematical thought, which had such a natural
attraction for Plato and in many important respects determined
the direction of his speculations. Those of us who knew Cornford
at that time can only marvel at the completeness with which all
this in itself indigestible material was assimilated and transmuted,
so that the reader who is presented with the finished commentary
can scarcely be aware of the amount of patient labour that has gone
to its composition.

The later dialogues of Plato will never attract more than a
limited circle of readers. It is otherwise with the *Republic*, and by
making his last published work a new translation of that central
dialogue he put a much wider public in his debt. His aim was to
ensure that this version would produce on the Greekless but otherwise educated Englishman as nearly as possible the same effect as
the original produced on the contemporary Greek. To this end he
took, as he said, 'certain liberties', which in his opinion 'it was
reasonable to suppose that Plato would have sanctioned in an
edition prepared for the modern press'. One of the most obvious
of these was to ignore in a number of passages the convention
whereby the development of the argument of Socrates is constantly interrupted by formal interjections of assent on the part of
his hearers. The convention is alien to English prose, and it cannot
be denied that by this and similar devices a real barrier has been
removed from between Plato and a modern reader. The value of
the book as part of a general education received welcome and
perhaps unexpected recognition when the Army Education
authorities selected it for their syllabus.

In Cornford's younger days the crying need for reform in certain aspects of University teaching put him definitely on the side of his own 'Young Men in a Hurry' against any middle-aged upholders of the *status quo*, and he wrote the satire *Microcosmographia Academica* (1908) whose truth has been found to extend well beyond the academic sphere. Civil servants and business men alike have claimed to recognise in their own walks of life the types which it portrays. In his later years I do not think he was by nature a controversialist, yet he found himself forced to take the field against some who, as it seemed to him, would not let the Greeks speak for themselves. Instead of trying to understand them by inquiring what were the problems of their own day to which they were seeking answers, these scholars were interpreting them in terms of present-day problems and present-day conflicts. Thus the Ionian philosophers and Epicurus became politically-minded scientists, who in addition to producing purely rational explanations of the physical universe were concerned to see these explanations offered to the masses in place of the religious ideas which were being perpetuated to bolster up the interests of a reactionary class. In this argument Plato appears as the champion of reaction. Politically, Cornford was the reverse of an oligarch. (This is not the place to go into his political views, which he did not consider relevant to his search for the truth about the Greeks, but it may be mentioned that his standpoint was that of a Fabian socialist.) Yet in the interests of truth he felt bound to protest when the haughty and oracular Heracleitus, who condemned inquiry and claimed to have found wisdom by looking into his own mind, was impressed into the ranks of experimental scientists, or when the class in Plato's *Republic* which included all holders of private wealth was described as the toiling masses. The notes which he has left behind suggest that he would have liked to express himself further on this subject. It has therefore seemed right to include in this volume the one essay, hitherto unpublished, which he devoted to it.

It is not every classical scholar whom one can commend to the reader not only for his matter but for the beauty of his writing and the art with which his works are composed. This also therefore should be mentioned in speaking of Cornford, but briefly, since to learn that a book or an essay is a work of art it is better to read it than to read about it. His art has itself a Hellenic quality, which would not call for comment in one who spent most of his life in such close touch with many aspects of Greek culture, were it not in fact comparatively rare among such men. To read him brings from time to time the same flooding pleasure that I myself get from the *Phaedo*, and others from contemplating the form and decoration of a Greek vase. All the main qualities are there, the living (not mechanical) symmetry of form, the grace and delicacy of the details, the humour, irony and occasional fantasy enlivening a fundamentally serious theme. This is a heavy-handed description, but if anyone thinks it at the same time extravagant, I commend to him the essay in the present volume called *The Harmony of the Spheres*.

I am only concerned here with Cornford as a writer on scholarly subjects, leaving to others who knew him intimately the more difficult task of portraying him in the round. All I would add is that in trying to crystallise my own impressions I find two Homeric epithets constantly recurring to my mind as together providing the best summing-up:

φίλος τ' ἦν αἰδοῖός τε.

W. K. C. G.

PETERHOUSE,
CAMBRIDGE

11 November 1949

NOTE

THE essay 'The Unconscious Element in Literature and Philosophy' was read to the Classical Association in 1921, and printed in its *Proceedings* for that year. That on 'Plato's Commonwealth' appeared in *Greece and Rome*, vol. IV (1935). Thanks are due to the Council of the Classical Association and the editors of *Greece and Rome* for permission to reprint these two. The essay 'Greek Natural Philosophy and Modern Science' was originally a contribution to the symposium *Background to Modern Science*, published by the Cambridge University Press in 1938. The other essays in this book have not been printed before.

The essays are printed in chronological order. I have chosen to name the third one on the title-page, because if, as Cornford said, it sometimes seemed to him that he had all his life been writing the same book, the title of that symbolic volume might well be said to be 'The Unwritten Philosophy'.

W. K. C. G.

THE UNCONSCIOUS ELEMENT IN LITERATURE AND PHILOSOPHY

I AM inviting you to consider the unconscious element in literature and philosophy, because it has lately occurred to me that that is what I have always been thinking and writing about. I have observed too that, in so far as my work in any department of ancient literature attracts notice, the result has been to provoke in the specialists in that department a feeling for which the mildest name is disgust; whereas students in other departments sometimes show symptoms of satisfaction. That phenomenon admits of more than one explanation. The most flattering (which I naturally prefer) is that, if you direct attention to those factors in an author's work which are in any sense unconscious, you strike the specialist as detracting from those merits which the author may be supposed to have valued most highly. If he is an historian, you seem to undermine his credibility; if a dramatist, you seem to belittle his deliberate craftsmanship; if a philosopher, you seem to deny his originality.

I think there is a misunderstanding here, which I should be glad to clear up. I have mainly in view the early Greek philosophers; but I will say a word first about history and drama.

To begin with Thucydides. Long ago I wrote a book with the provocative title *Thucydides Mythistoricus*. I did not mean to challenge Thucydides' claim to be perhaps the most trustworthy of all historians. My thesis did not necessarily cast a doubt upon any single statement of objective fact. But it seemed to me that any historian's choice of facts to be recorded, his distribution of emphasis among them, his sense of their significance and relative proportion, must be governed by his philosophy of life. For the history of the Peloponnesian War, Thucydides is our only authority of the first rank. How are we to control his presentation of the facts? In such a case criticism can apply only one method. It consists in disengaging from the narrative that whole framework of preconception which the author cannot help bringing with him, because it is the very atmosphere of his mind—in a word, his philosophy of life. In Thucydides this element may be called unconscious, in a loose and popular sense, in that he made an heroic effort to keep objective fact in the focal centre of his attention. He was aware, moreover, of the seductions of party bias and personal passion. Such factors obtrude themselves from time to time within the field of attention; they can be detected and deliberately suppressed. But, enveloping and pervading the whole area of the mind, like a subtle and penetrating ether, there is a man's philosophy of life—a factor which does not obtrude itself at any particular moment, for the reason that it is always and everywhere present. In order to detect it, to guard against it, he would have to go outside himself. No note of warning comes to him from the objective world. Everyone knows, from his own experience, that there is no fact so brutish and unmalleable as not to fit into the frame of his philosophy; otherwise philosophy would sometimes have to yield to facts, and where would any philosophy be then? It is of the nature of philosophy to claim objective validity. In the same way, to the ordinary man nothing seems more certainly objective than space. Yet Kant declared that space was only a pure form of our intuition—a form contributed by our minds. A philosophy of life is analogous to Kantian space. Really contributed by our minds, it is innocently projected into the external world. The most cautious and honest historian cannot free himself from the laws of his optical perspective. The objective facts he is looking for present themselves already embedded in this setting, ordered by its symmetry, dyed by its colours.

But it is possible for us, who look at Thucydides' world from a different angle through glasses of a different power and hue, to make out the subjective character of this philosophy. Our first business as critics should be to disengage it and to study it in isolation. Then we may see how it would bend the course of the narrative at any point; in what patterns it would tend to group the facts; how it would throw the light upon some, and leave others in the shade.

Now this is not to say that Thucydides' philosophy of life is not, vithin its limits, a true philosophy—as true as any alternative our own minds may contribute. It may even be truer. Fourteen years ago, writing under the impression of the South African war, I may have overstressed the financial aspect of imperialism. Since 1914 Thucydides' moral interpretation of history has seemed more profound. But that does not touch the main thesis, namely, that there are alternative interpretations; that each is limited and tends to obscure the truth contained in the others; and that the criticism of an ancient historian should begin with the study of his *a priori* forms of thought, fashioned in a time when economic science, for instance, was not invented.

I turn next to the Drama. Here the case is different. No critic can overlook the philosophies of Aeschylus, Sophocles, Euripides; nor is there here any question of disentangling the philosophies in order to arrive at objective fact. The unconscious element in drama falls under two heads: (*a*) the traditional form, (*b*) the myth.

(*a*) The traditional form of ancient drama may be called an unconscious factor in the sense that it is accepted without a thought, as a painter accepts his canvas.[1] The painter's mind is intent on his design; the dramatist's on the contrivance of the detailed variable plot which he will fit into the given frame. But the frame is there; and unless you disengage it and allow for it, you cannot fully measure the skill with which the dramatist has turned it to account. Nor can I see anything indecent or impertinent in the attempt to explain why the frame is there. I refer, of course, to Professor Murray's theory that the 'fixed forms' of Attic Tragedy correspond to the moments in a ritual drama which survives all over Europe in the folk-play. Some good scholars have approved this theory; others, for some cause I cannot quite fathom, are reduced by it to a state of frenzy; others, again, think that there may be some truth in it, but that it is irrelevant, if not uninteresting. To this last class belong scholars of the type of my own great master, Arthur Verrall; and perhaps I may add his worthy successor, Mr Sheppard, whose brilliant powers as a literary critic are

---

[1] In so far as the traditional form, if really a ritual form, carries with it the associations of the ritual myth, what is said below about myth becomes relevant here.

reinforced by an artist's mastery of stagecraft. He, too, is mainly interested in the conscious and deliberate art of the poets and in their philosophic reflection. That is a field wide enough for the display of the finest critical faculty, and when a Verrall or a Sheppard displays it I am eager to join in the applause. Only I wonder whether it is the whole field. When Mr Sheppard demonstrates the existence of a personal Homer from the evidence of design in the *Iliad* and *Odyssey*, my thoughts wander to Archdeacon Paley. Bergson explains how it is that the intellect can always find inexhaustible evidence of design in creation, which, nevertheless (he thinks), had no designer. In poetic creation there may be a great deal of design; but I suggest that there is always less than the cleverest critic can find evidence for—sometimes much less. Creation is not all or mainly contrivance; some of its happiest effects occur at points where the freedom of its flow is checked or turned in an unforeseen direction by the limits of given material or of traditional form. This is one of the ways in which luck favours art, and art has reason to delight in luck.

(*b*) So much for the framework of traditional form. Consider next the tragic plots that are fitted into this frame. Our word 'plot' pre-eminently suggests contrivance and the interest of intrigue, kept in a state of tension until it is released by an unforeseen denouement. The plots of the New Comedy are of this kind; but it is a commonplace that this interest of intrigue is foreign to Greek tragedy. We find there primarily not the 'plot' but the myth. Now if we take the Oedipus myth, for example; if we forget what Sophocles has made of it, and then judge it merely as a story, an anecdote of early Theban history, it will seem repulsive and hardly deserving of a place in literature of any higher kind than the *Police Court News*. The few belated adherents of Euhemerus may be content to take it so; but most of us will feel that the great myths of the world are more than historical anecdotes. They come, even to us, charged with a congenial warmth, with the appeal of a mysterious significance lying behind their face value as legendary incident. We are, very dimly but intensely, aware of some universal meaning that is contained in a myth, and not contained in a plot of intrigue. And we must be right in supposing that the race which preserved these myths while it forgot its national history, and the dramatists who preferred to use them rather than invent new stories, must also have felt, in their different ways and degrees, this same peculiar quality, and have valued it, however little they could account for its presence.

Now in recent times comparative anthropology, directed upon classical material by the illustrious author of the *Golden Bough*, has swept away all the earlier keys to mythology by interpreting the myths in terms of social institutions of the prehistoric past. It will hardly be denied nowadays that this work has extended our comprehension of the myths; but it is challenged by the criticism that these prehistoric institutions had been forgotten by the Greeks themselves, and that consequently all this enlargement of *our* comprehension is irrelevant to the interpretation of Aeschylus or Sophocles. You can dispose of it by remarking that Aeschylus had never visited Melanesia and Sophocles had never read the *Golden Bough*. Mr Sheppard practically says as much in his learned and subtle book on the *Oedipus Tyrannus*. He writes there:[1]

The origin and early history of the [Oedipus] myth I do not discuss. Modern theories are based on inadequate evidence and very bold hypotheses. Even if they could be proved, they would be irrelevant here *unless it could be established that they were known to Athenians of the time of Sophocles.* For this reason I have nothing to say about 'medicine-kings', vegetation-spirits, marriage with the earth-mother.

Mr Sheppard's reason could not be more conclusive. No one can ever establish that 'modern theories' were known to Athenians in the time of Sophocles.

But I understand Mr Sheppard's point: he says 'modern theories' because he will not say 'modern knowledge'. And, even granted that the knowledge gained from comparative study *is* knowledge, he thinks that we know too much—far more about primitive religion than the fifth-century Greeks knew—and that we read back that knowledge into the plays illegitimately, and so invest them with a significance they did not possess for their authors and spectators.

[1] P. xviii, footnote; my italics.

Frankly, I admit that Professor Murray and we who in the main think with him do sometimes fall into that error. On the other hand, it seems to me a less serious error than the opposite one of assuming that the whole religious background of the myths and traditional mould of Greek tragedy had been, in Sophocles' time, irrecoverably blotted out of the memory of the Greek race. The ancients certainly knew about the earth-mother. They may have understood more about divine kings and even vegetation-spirits than Mr Sheppard chooses to allow; for, after all, the 'bold hypotheses' of Sir James Frazer or Miss Jane Harrison, in so far as they apply to classical antiquity, are based entirely on evidence supplied by the ancients themselves.

Grant, however, that the ancients had little explicit knowledge; grant that Aeschylus himself would have had much to learn about Zeus from Mr Arthur Cook,—that does not settle the question. How can any modern critic be positive that, in that fantastic region of the mind where concrete images take the place of discursive thought, there were not still links of association, however obscure and unexplicit, connecting (say) the figure of Jocasta with the earth-mother, and the figure of Oedipus with the divine king? We are assured that the individual mind, though in one sense it forgets all but a tiny fraction of its experience, in another sense never forgets anything—not even experience of which it was not, at the time, aware. Similarly, the memory of a race, enshrined in a continuous tradition of myth, legend, poetry, retains knowledge which, after a sufficient lapse of time, no individual can formulate in abstract terms. The knowledge is not blotted out, though you may say it is forgotten; it lives on in symbol and image, and finally, as it were, fossilised in metaphor, as a system linked together by chords of association that vibrate without the interposition of rational, directed thinking. Our view is that modern research into origins is not only recovering the temporal sequence of the several stages in the development of religious representations, but is also, by that very fact, bringing to light the corresponding systems of association deposited, at those stages, in the racial tradition and memory of the Greeks—systems that lasted on in their minds like the superimposed layers of alluvial stratification. *It is from these hidden layers that the springs of poetry rise.* That is why Greek poetry is full of passages that for us become enriched with meaning when read in the light of new discoveries. What we attribute to Sophocles is not acquaintance with 'modern theories', not the explicit knowledge of the prehistoric past, but the latent systems of unconscious association, ultimately derived from that past, and not so deeply buried but that the images composing them can emerge in the fabric of poetic creation.

But there is yet another answer which goes deeper and suggests that these systems of unconscious association are even now not wholly lost. This answer is furnished by the psychological interpretation of myth.

On the one hand, you have, persisting in the time of Aeschylus and Sophocles, and reverently regarded by them, a great mass of ritual practice. We can see that, in the case of a substantial part of this ritual, the meaning had involved such ideas as marriage with the earth-mother, or participation in the barely personified life of all nature, inadequately named 'the vegetation-spirit'. The rituals, as living social institutions, expressed these ideas in the concrete form of action. On the other hand, you have the myths, which appear to us to involve the same set of ideas, expressed this time in words, and disguised by the concrete form of legendary narrative, professing to be the history of prehistoric men and women. What is the link between these two forms of expression, or methods of symbolism—the ritual and the narrative, the social institution and the myth?

The psychological interpretation asserts that behind both these alternative symbolisms there lies the universal inner experience of human beings—experience that is never antiquated, but repeated in every generation, and not confined to Melanesia, or to Athens, or to modern England. This experience, which, in a great variety of degrees and shapes, besets every new life that comes into the world to confront the task of adapting itself to what it finds there, is the ultimate common factor shared by us with Sophocles, and by Sophocles and us with those remoter ancestors who transmitted the symbolical expression of the universal problems of life and their solutions. It is the perennial existence of this experience, the recurrent pressure of the same problems, the recurrent need of the same solutions, that explains (as nothing else explains) that mysterious quality of appeal which, as I said, the myth contains, and the anecdote or artificial plot does not contain. The myth makes this appeal directly and universally, because, like the corresponding religious ritual, it symbolises what does happen, and what ought to happen, and what ought not to happen, in the inner development of any human life. That is, in the last resort, the reason why a play like the *Oedipus* is to us, not a stiff, archaic monument of a bygone age, but a living thing that shakes every nerve in our moral being. That is the ground of our assurance that we not only understand Sophocles but feel with him.

I do not know to what extent students of classical mythology have attended to the results obtained by the analytical psychologists of Vienna and Zürich. Consequently, I do not know whether what I have just said sounds in most ears as a platitude or as an unintelligible absurdity. In the hope that it sounds familiar, I will only indicate its bearing on my subject.

The psychological interpretation explains the fact, which has long been known, that certain mythical themes or motives, fundamentally the same though overlaid with endless variety of detail, are found in the legends and folk-tales of peoples so widely scattered over the globe that the alternative hypothesis of migration from one original centre becomes extremely difficult. The migration hypothesis should, no doubt, be pressed as far as ethnological discovery will warrant; no one denies that migration occurs. But, if its fullest claims were conceded, the question would remain, why some myths spread everywhere and others do not. Here psychology would step in, and by the analysis of these universal myths would show that, if they are borrowed, it is because they are wanted—because they satisfy some need and symbolise some experience that were already there and waiting for this expression. Between the two hypotheses there is no necessary conflict.

Dr Jung, however, would go further. The study of the unconscious contents of contemporary minds is bringing to light the fact—however it is to be explained—that people to-day, in their dreams, use the symbolism of the primitive mythical themes, such as rebirth, death, and resurrection, eating the god, and so on—symbolism that often coincides in surprising detail with the universal myths, so that the myth can be interpreted from the dream, and the dream from the myth. The dreams containing this symbolism appear to refer to typical conflicts which constantly occur in the psychical development of individuals, and, moreover, to point to solutions of these conflicts, to indicate the direction in which the psychic energy that is being wasted in them might be set free in a normal adaptation to the demands of life.

Further, this primitive symbolism seems to lie in a very deep stratum of the unconscious mind, below the contents of the 'personal unconscious', as Dr Jung calls it. By the personal unconscious he means those contents which can be identified as buried memories of individual experience—events that have happened to the individual and been forgotten. Below these is that deeper stratum, the contents of which seem to Dr Jung not to be traceable to individual experience, but to consist of the universal primitive symbolism. He calls this the 'impersonal' or 'collective unconscious'. Whatever the explanation may be, it is *as if* the individual mind to-day passed through every phase in the development of the mind of the race, just as the embryo of the body is said to pass through the pre-human stages of evolution; and *as if* the individual mind preserved some memory, normally quite inaccessible to the waking consciousness, of every phase of imagery and symbolism which the mind of the race has used in its progress to abstract conceptual thought.

If this conception should turn out to be valid, the rather exorbitant demand for proof that 'modern theories' were known in fifth-century Athens ceases to have any point at all. If the symbolism, for instance, of marriage with the earth-mother is actually present now in all our minds, including Mr Sheppard's, we may assume that it was present in the mind of Sophocles, and probably much nearer the surface. The appeal of that symbolism disguised in the Oedipus myth would help to invest what is otherwise merely a revolting story with that mysterious quality which would make it worthy to be chosen as a tragic theme.

In this section of my paper dealing with the myth, the word 'unconscious' has been used in a sense not applicable to the historian's or the poet's philosophy of life. This is not contributed by what the psychologists call 'the unconscious'. But the myth is a different thing. The myth is like a tree whose leaves and flowers in the upper air of the conscious mind are sustained by a root that stretches down, out of sight, into the unconscious levels. The tree is fed, from age to age, by a vital sap welling up from that root in a secret and perennial flow.

Finally there is the case of philosophy. I know that to speak of an unconscious element in philosophy is to outrage the feelings of philosophers. Yet I am convinced that, until it is recognised, the history of thought cannot be written in full.

Professor Burnet, in the last edition of his *Early Greek Philosophy*—a work to which every student must acknowledge a deep obligation—remarks in a footnote that 'the fundamental error of Mr Cornford's interesting book *From Religion to Philosophy*' is the error of 'deriving science from mythology'. I have failed, it seems, to realise that 'Ionia was a country without a past', and that 'there was no traditional background there at all'. If Professor Burnet is right, my error is so fundamental that his complimentary epithet 'interesting' should be withdrawn. My book is of no interest whatever unless science is, in some sense, 'derived from mythology'. I think myself that the error did not lie there, but in the failure to make it perfectly clear how this 'derivation' is to be conceived. Perhaps I can make it clearer now.

I cannot here examine Professor Burnet's strange statement that Ionia was a country without a past or a traditional background. This is sometimes said of the United States; but a history of American thought which refused to take any account of European religion and speculation before the sailing of the *Mayflower*, or even before the voyage of Columbus, would not go to the roots of the matter. I will not pursue the parallel, but only state my conviction that there never has been, on the surface of this planet, any set of human beings with no past and no traditional background. And philosophy is the work of human beings, not of countries. I shall assume, then, that the minds of the Ionian philosophers were not pure intelligences, absolutely vacant, and presenting to the external world the placard 'To be let unfurnished'.

I will illustrate my point from the system of Anaximander. Time will allow me to consider only one point in that system; but that is the central point—the primordial stuff of the universe, that 'unlimited' nature from which all individual existence emerges, and into which it returns. This world-stuff is described as without beginning or end, ageless and deathless, divine. It has some of the properties we ascribe to matter; but its most essential property is one that we commonly deny to unorganised matter, namely, life, and the inherent power of self-motion characteristic of the living. It is called, not 'matter'—the word was not yet invented—but 'God'. It is, as it were, a first approximation to that 'neutral stuff', not yet differentiated into 'mind' and 'matter', which is emerging once more in American philosophy.

Where does this concept, or (as I should prefer to call it) this *image*, come from? That is a question to be faced and answered. It is not answered, nor even faced, in any history of philosophy I am acquainted with.

Was it deliberately fabricated by Anaximander? I think not. It is true that the modern physicist may be said to fabricate concepts, such as the ether, by refining and recombining older concepts, and putting together into an arbitrary collection the determinate properties he requires, and only those. He proceeds thus deliberately, because centuries of critical reflection have taught him that such a concept is only hypothetical, not given; therefore he feels free to adapt it in any way that will fit it to support the phenomena he has observed. But this entire method is modern. Anaximander did not start from observation and proceed to construct an hypothesis. He started with a problem beyond the range of any possible observation—the origin of the world. And his image of the primordial nature of things was announced with all the confidence of prophetic dogma, because it presented itself to him with all the authority of an intuitive vision of the real. He did not go about to make it; it came to him as given. Whence did it come?

It was certainly not given, through the senses, by the external world. It must, therefore, have been given by some part of the philosopher's mind.

Now when an image (as distinct from an object of sensation) presents itself to our consciousness as given, as independent of our will, authoritative and objectively valid, that may mean one of two things. It may mean that the image, or concept, or belief, is part of our social tradition, which we have been taught and remember. The authoritative character is then due to the sanction of the collective mind of our group. This applies to our moral ideas and beliefs; but it does not apply to the case before us. This image of a single living divine stuff was not, so far as we know, a traditional representation in Ionia, imposed by authority.

I do not see how to avoid falling back on the second alternative, offered by modern psychology. This is the view that an image such as we are concerned with emerges from a level of the unconscious mind so deep that we do not recognise it as part of ourselves. I mean Dr Jung's collective unconscious.

'In every individual,' says Dr Jung, 'in addition to the personal memories, there are also, in Jacob Burckhardt's excellent phrase, the great "primordial images", the inherited potentialities of human imagination. They have always been potentially latent in the structure of the brain. The fact of this inheritance also explains the otherwise incredible phenomenon, that the matter and themes of certain legends are met with all the world over in identical forms. Further, it explains how it is that persons who are mentally deranged are able to produce precisely the same images and associations that are known to us from the study of old manuscripts.... I do not hereby assert the *transmission of representations*, but only of the *possibility of such representations*, which is a very different thing.'[1]

In my book I adopted, with some trepidation, the suggestion of MM. Hubert and Mauss that the Ionian image of the nature of things—this living stuff—could be connected with the primitive image of *Mana*. But I could not then see how the connection could be established. It is plainly not a case either of overt tradition or

[1] *Analytical Psychology* (English trans.), 2nd ed. (1920), p. 410.

of migration. Dr Jung independently brings the same two images together and he provides the link. On this view *Mana* and *physis* are varieties—though varieties that differ in important respects—of the same 'primordial image', upon which (as he says) 'primitive religions, in the most dissimilar regions of the earth, are founded'. I believe that both are images of the psychic energy itself—of that life-force which every sentient creature feels as the driving-power within it.

No doubt Dr Jung's concept of the collective unconscious may be susceptible of further analysis. If it proves valid, it will lead to the conclusion that the development of philosophy and science centrally consists in the differentiation, under the action of conscious intellectual criticism, of these primordial images which had, by a different process, previously given birth to every form of religious representation. The image presents itself at first as a confused complex of properties, natural and mystical, subjective and objective. The work of philosophy is to analyse this mass, and to cut out of it a number of clear and more determinate concepts, which become the tools of science. It is not the case that philosophy or science is immediately 'derived' from mythology. Both are derived, by different channels, from the same source in the impersonal unconscious.

THE HARMONY OF THE SPHERES

Lorenzo (to Jessica)
> Sweet soul, let's in, and there expect their coming.
> And yet no matter—why should we go in?
> My friend Stephano, signify, I pray you,
> Within the house, your mistress is at hand;
> And bring your music forth into the air.
> How sweet the moonlight sleeps upon this bank!
> Here will we sit, and let the sounds of music
> Creep in our ears: soft stillness and the night
> Becomes the touches of sweet harmony.
>
> Sit, Jessica; look, how the floor of heaven
> Is thick inlaid with patines of bright gold:
> There's not the smallest orb which thou behold'st
> But in his motion like an angel sings;
> Still quiring to the young-eyed cherubins;
> Such harmony is in immortal souls;
> But whilst this muddy vesture of decay
> Doth grossly close it in, we cannot hear it....

Jessica   I am never merry when I hear sweet music.

Lorenzo   The reason is, your spirits are attentive:
> For do but note a wild and wanton herd,
> Or race of youthful and unhandled colts,
> Fetching mad bounds, bellowing and neighing loud,
> Which is the hot condition of their blood;
> If they but hear perchance a trumpet sound,
> Or any air of music touch their ears,
> You shall perceive them make a mutual stand,
> Their savage eyes turned to a modest gaze
> By the sweet power of music. Therefore the poet
> Did feign that Orpheus drew trees, stones, and floods;
> Since nought so stockish, hard, and full of rage
> But music for the time doth change his nature.
> The man that hath no music in himself,
> Nor is not moved with concord of sweet sounds,
> Is fit for treasons, stratagems, and spoils;
> The motions of his spirit are dull as night,

And his affections dark as Erebus:
Let no such man be trusted.

Jessica (no answer)
Lorenzo Mark the music.

Consider this scene: the dark avenue leading to Portia's hall of Belmont; the gentle wind in the trees; the moonlight falling on the new-married lovers; above them the night sky and the stars. I say the stars, although in the only commentary I could lay hands on, I read, with a shock, that Lorenzo, when he spoke of patines of bright gold inlaid in the floor of heaven, 'was probably referring to the small broken clouds preluding the dawn'—as if clouds could be inlaid in a floor; or as if, on such a night, there could be clouds in the Venetian sky over-arching the happiness of so many lovers. Reading further, I was reassured as to the sanity of at least some scholars: 'some believe the reference to be to the orbs of heaven'. These, no doubt, had taken the trouble to read the next line: 'There's not the smallest orb which thou behold'st'; so much profit is to be gained by the critic scanning the context through his spectacles, though his imagination may have no inward eye. Jessica, at any rate, looking up at the majestical roof, would need no Hamlet to tell her that it was fretted with golden fires, not gilded clouds—fires, moreover, that were not yet paling before the dawn, but growing brighter as the setting moon sank to sleep with Endymion. Some minutes earlier, before Stephano brought news that Portia would be home before daybreak, Jessica's wits had been lively enough to match his Cressida and Dido with Thisbe and Medea, for she had read Ovid in some Italian version; but now she is lying back on the grass, while Lorenzo charms her to a mood of quietness, discoursing on the unheard harmonies of heaven. She sinks deeper into a dream, as first the words, and then the strains of music, creep in her ear, like the sweet sound that breathes upon a bank of violets, stealing and giving odour. The gaiety passes from her spirits—'I am never merry when I hear sweet music'—and she is content to be lulled by Lorenzo's eloquence and to let Time stand still.

But Time will not stand still, so long as we are awake, because the brain has more of the clock than the sundial—the clock that will measure each minute with insistent ticking. So, even in the suspense and all but slumber of the higher faculties (as we choose to call them), some wisps of thought must be drifting over the field of Jessica's consciousness. What is she thinking? She is not looking at the sky as she was told to do; she is watching her husband, while he sits propped on one hand and gazing, not at the stars nor yet at her, but into the level distance. 'Dear Lorenzo. How familiar and strange he looks in the moonlight, and how much he knows about the stars. It is time we went in to prepare a welcome for Portia. He was telling me so only a moment since. But then he said "and yet no matter, why should we go in?" and sent for the musicians to come out and play to us. So be it; no matter, then; Portia is in love herself and she will surely forgive us. It is good to lie here and listen to him talking about—what is he talking about?'

For Lorenzo's voice has come to a pause. Looking down, he sees why no answer is forthcoming; but courteous and, after all, newly married, he only tells her to mark the music, without adding 'if you cannot mark me'. But we must not find fault with Jessica; if the thinking part of her mind has dwindled to so small a measure, that is because all the rest of her consciousness is drowned in the still tide of feeling. She has taken into every recess of her being that harmony of earthly and heavenly music which Lorenzo's eager mind is bent upon describing in words. The meaning of the words she has ceased to heed; but they have borne a part in creating the peace of her experience.

And what has been happening in Lorenzo's mind? His eye is fixed on the candle lighted in a window of the Hall to guide its mistress home; but he does not see the candle. The influence of the stars and the moonlight is upon him too; the music fills his hearing; but if music be the food of love for Jessica, for Lorenzo at this moment it is also the food of thought. He is thinking of all he has learnt of the legend of Orpheus and the mathematical philosophy of Pythagoras—topics remote enough from Jessica, who, if she had ever heard of Pythagoras, probably was like Malvolio and knew no more of him than his opinion concerning wildfowl: that the soul of our grandam might haply inhabit a bird. And what (she might have asked, if she had been listening at all) has that to do with the quiring orbs? Or what, for that matter, have the orbs themselves to do with the young-eyed cherubins? The cherubins, my commentary says, are 'introduced in allusion to Job 38. 7', though in point of fact they are not mentioned there, but only the morning stars which sang together. We might be tempted to see in Lorenzo's admixture of Hebrew myth with Greek astronomy a delicate acknowledgment of Jessica's Jewish birth; and if it was wasted on her, Lorenzo would not have cared. But I would sooner think that he had read the *Paradiso*, and learnt that the Cherubim, at the inner rim of the crystalline heaven, are next-neighbours to the heaven of the fixed stars, and first of the angelic hierarchy to hear the symphony of the planetary spheres.

Be that as it may, certainly Lorenzo was more deeply instructed than his wife. We know nothing of him but that he was a gentleman, and in Launcelot's judgment no good member of the commonwealth, in that by converting Jews to Christians he was raising the price of pork. But he must have been a student at the University of Padua, and (I am tempted to add) there learnt more than Shakespeare knew about Pythagoras and Orpheus. If you will imagine yourselves in the Paduan School of Astronomy and Music, I will try to reconstruct the store of learning on which Lorenzo drew. I shall enjoy the freedom of speaking as a Paduan professor from the chair later to be filled by Galileo; but I promise you not to repeat what, as a member of another university, I believe to be untrue.

In the island of Samos, towards the middle of the sixth century before Christ, Pythagoras was born. In early manhood he removed to southern Italy, and there founded a brotherhood, with some monastic features, which lasted for about two hundred years—through the lifetimes of Socrates, Plato, and Aristotle—and left a tradition which was still living in the earliest Christian centuries. Of his life we know little more; and that for a significant reason. Already by his immediate followers he was recognised (like his contemporary, the Buddha) as one of those divine men of whom history knows least because their lives are at once transfigured into legend. He was, they said, the son of a God, Apollo, by a mortal woman; and Aristotle recorded some of the miracles ascribed to his more than human powers. His doctrines are commonly classed under two heads: the religious and the scientific or philosophical; but in fact they are only parts of a single vision of the universe.

The soul is of its own nature immortal, that is to say divine. When the body dies, the soul, according to its deeds, passes into other forms of life, of man or animal or plant. It is bound upon this wheel of reincarnation until it shall have become pure. It will then regain a place in the company of the immortal gods and heroes. The body is no better than a temporary prison-house or tomb of the living soul, thus grossly closed in the muddy vesture of decay. From this follows the unity of all life: there is a bond of kinship uniting man to the gods above him and the beasts below: for any soul may climb or descend to any rung upon the single ladder of existence. And the sin for which the fallen soul has been condemned to its round of mortal births was a breach of this unity, symbolised by the shedding of blood.

Reincarnation had been taught earlier by the votaries of Orpheus, who were banded in mystical cult-societies in Pythagoras' adopted country, South Italy. They too abstained from killing animals or eating flesh, holding the same belief that the unity of life should be inviolate. Upon secret sympathy between all creatures had rested the power of Orpheus, who, for them as for us, was a figure of the far legendary past. He was the enchanting son of the Muse Calliope; and his enchantment was wrought by music, the sober Apolline music of the lyre:

> Such notes as, warbled to the string,
> Drew iron tears down Pluto's cheek
> And made Hell grant what love did seek.

But all this is a familiar theme in English poetry.

Now the myth of Orpheus contains a thought that took shape in the mind of Pythagoras. How can music possess this magical influence? If the power of music is felt by all living things, and even (as Lorenzo says) by trees, stones, and floods, there must be in the principle of life itself, in the soul of man and of universal nature, chords that can answer to the touch of harmonious sound. May it not be the most essential truth about the soul that it is, in some sort, an instrument of music?

Tradition, truly as I believe, reports that Pythagoras declared the soul to be, or to contain, a harmony—or rather a *harmonia*. For in Greek the word *harmonia* does not mean 'harmony', if 'harmony' conveys to us the concord of several sounds. The Greeks called that *symphonia*. *Harmonia* meant originally the orderly adjustment of parts in a complex fabric; then, in particular, the tuning of a musical instrument; and finally the musical scale, composed of several notes yielded by the tuned strings. What we call the 'modes' would be to the Greek *harmoniai*.

Pythagoras turned to the study of the musical scales; and in this field he made a discovery which gave him a clue to the whole structure of the world. He found that the concordant intervals of the musical scale can be exactly expressed in terms of ratios between numbers. It was only later that Greek musicians guessed that these ratios hold between the numbers of vibrations corresponding to the several notes. Pythagoras simply measured the lengths on the string of a monochord, stopped by a movable bridge. It came to light that the ratio of the octave is $1:2$; of the fourth, $4:3$; of the fifth, $3:2$. These (which are still known to musicians as the 'perfect consonances') are the fixed intervals common to all the Greek scales, the variety of scales being obtained by varying the intervening or 'movable' notes. Observe further that the numbers which occur in these ratios are 1, 2, 3, 4—the sum of which is 10, the perfect number. Pythagoras would never have made the experiment, if he had not already divined that the order and beauty evoked by the art of music from the weltering chaos of sound—a matter, plainly enough, of measure, proportion, rhythm—might be reducible to the pure abstractions of number. To discover that these fundamental proportions, on which every scale is built, could be expressed so simply in ratios between the first four numbers was enough to flood any mathematician's soul with joy. To Pythagoras it came as a revelation, lighting up the framework of the moral, no less than of the natural, world.

First, in the microcosm of the individual, not only are strength and beauty dependent on proportions and rhythms of form, of which the Greek sculptors might determine the canon, but health—the virtue of the body—was interpreted as a proportion or equipoise of contending elements, which any excess might derange or finally destroy. And virtue—the health of the soul—likewise lay in the golden mean, imposing measure on the turbulence of passion, a temperance which excludes both excess and deficiency. In virtue the soul achieves moral order and beauty; its *harmonia* is in tune.

> Dust as we are, the immortal spirit grows
> Like harmony in music, there is a dark
> Inscrutable workmanship that reconciles
> Discordant elements, makes them cling together
> In one society.

That the soul should be harmonised meant not only that its several parts should be in tune with one another, but, as one instrument in an orchestra must be in tune with all the rest, so the soul must reproduce the *harmonia* of the Cosmos. The phrase 'in tune with the infinite' is one that no musician, least of all a Greek musician, would use. The very essence of order is a measure or limit imposed upon the infinite or unlimited; and looking out into the world of Nature, Pythagoras saw here the secret of beauty and of rational truth.

For in the field of the eye, no less than of the ear, there is harmony or discord in the relations of colour, and there is measure and proportion in form. Music has its being in time, not in space; but space is peopled with extended bodies having surfaces whose shapes and colours, confounded in the darkness, are, as it were, recreated daily by the dawn of light. From the measurement of these surfaces we can reach the theorems of geometry, simple, perfect, and unalterably true. Moreover, the truths of geometry can be yet more abstractly expressed in numbers. So numbers and their properties and relations underlie the whole fabric of the world in space and time; and Pythagoras, in the language of his day, declared that numbers—not formless matter—were the 'nature of all things'.

It was Pythagoras who first gave to the visible world the name of Cosmos, a word which equally signifies order and beauty. Of his cosmogony only a few traces survive. These indicate that the two great principles of Nature are Light and Darkness, concretely conceived as Fire and the dark, cold vapour of primaeval Night filling the abyss of space. Imagine a spark or seed of Fire planted in the womb of unlimited Darkness. By the self-propagating power of light spreading outwards from this centre, a spherical realm of order and form and colour is won from the dominion of Night. This is the universe, the Cosmos, extending from earth at the centre to the sphere of the fixed stars. Between centre and circumference, the seven known planets (including sun and moon) are set, each like a jewel in its ring, in material orbits which carry them round; and these are spaced according to the intervals of a musical scale, the celestial *harmonia*.

The Pythagoreans suppose, says Aristotle, that the motion of bodies so huge as these and moving with so great a speed must produce a sound. Arguing so, and from the observation that their speeds, as measured by their distances, are in the same ratios as the concords of the musical scale, they assert that the sound given forth by the revolution of the heavenly bodies is a *harmonia* or scale. They explain that we do not hear this music because the sound is constantly in our ears from the very moment of birth and so cannot be distinguished by contrast with silence.

Such, in its earliest form, is the harmony of the spheres. 'The whole heaven', said the Pythagoreans, 'is harmony and number'—number because the essence of harmony lies, not in the sound, but in the numerical proportions, and these (I think we may add) constitute the soul of Nature, which thus, like the human soul, is itself a harmony. So the moral world is interfused with the physical. The harmony of heaven is perfect; but its counterpart in human souls is marred with imperfection and discord. This is what we call vice or evil. The attainment of that purity which is to release the soul at last from the wheel of incarnation, may now be construed as the reproduction, in the individual, of the cosmic harmony—the divine order of the world. Herein lies the secret of the power of music over the soul. Accordingly the learned Bishop Hooker (*Eccles. Polity*, v, 38), writing in defence of church music, drew his arguments in 'the last resort from Pythagoras:

Touching musical harmony, whether by instrument or by voice, it being but of high or low in sounds a due proportionable disposition, such notwithstanding is the force thereof, and so pleasing effects it hath in that very part of man which is most divine, that some have been thereby induced to think that the soul itself is, or hath in it Harmony; a thing which delighteth all ages and beseemeth all states; a thing as seasonable in grief as in joy; as decent being added unto actions of greatest weight and solemnity, as being used when men most sequester themselves from action.

The reason hereof is an admirable facility which Music hath to express and represent the mind, more inwardly than any other sensible mean, the very standing, rising and falling, the very steps and inflections every way, the turns and varieties of all passions whereunto the mind is subject; yea, so to imitate them that, whether it resemble unto us the same state wherein our minds already are, or a clean contrary, we are not more contentedly by the one confirmed, than changed and led away by the other. In Harmony the very image and character even of virtue and vice is perceived, the mind delighted with their resemblances, and brought, by having them often iterated, into a love of the things themselves.

Finally, the influence of the celestial harmony is absorbed and assimilated by the soul in contemplation (*theoria*). The soul in the presence of the Cosmos was compared to the spectator at a festival, who comes, not to compete for success or to traffic for gain, but to see and to enjoy. Contemplation is contrasted with practical activity. It was the gift of Mary, who chose the better part when Martha was cumbered with serving—Mary who, when Lazarus was dead, sat still in the house, while Martha went out to meet their guest. It was the gift of Rachel in Dante's dream on the Mount of Purgatory. Her sister Leah moves through the meadow to gather flowers; but Rachel sits all day at her mirror; Leah is satisfied with doing; but for Rachel it is enough to see. But if contemplation is not for practical ends, it is not merely passive, but (as Aristotle taught) an activity. To the Pythagorean it meant, not only taking in the spectacle of order and beauty in the visible heaven, but the active operation of thought in all the mathematical sciences which reveal the truths of number and form. Contemplation is the search for wisdom, not only the fruition. Among those whom the Greeks honoured as wise men, Pythagoras was the first to refuse the title and to call himself, not wise, but a lover of wisdom (*philo-sophos*), not a sage but a philosopher.

Such was the substance of the Paduan professor's discourse which came back to Lorenzo, and withdrew his mind into a world of speculation where Jessica could not follow. You will guess why I pushed my construction of that scene to a pitch that might seem overstrained. Which of the two has chosen the better part—Lorenzo, who sees neither the sky nor Jessica, but dwells in his mind's eye on the candle lighted by ancient wisdom in the darkness; or Jessica, content to watch her lover's eyes and to lie back dreaming on the earth, like Earth herself, all Danae to the stars?

The question is not easily answered. For the contrast between the two is not the contrast between Martha and Mary or Leah and Rachel. Both Lorenzo and Jessica have renounced and forgotten their immediate business of making ready for Portia the house she left in their charge. For this enchanted pause of contemplation they have sacrificed all duties of the practical life; even the musicians, posted in the Hall to greet their mistress, have been called forth into the air, as if to render audible to human ears the very tones of the quiring orbs. The choice lies rather between the active and the passive modes of contemplation. Does Lorenzo gain or lose by speculating upon the experience which Jessica is satisfied to enjoy, and spanning its depth with a structure of intellectual theory? There may be more than one answer to the question.

Two possible replies may be at once dismissed. The first I will call the brutal scientific reply: that the intellectual structure of Pythagorean cosmology is false to ascertained fact. We know that the earth does not stand still at the centre of a nest of revolving rings or spheres, carrying round the planets and fixed stars. For this and other reasons there can be no harmony of the spheres. The whole theory is an idle and obsolete fancy.

A second reply meets this criticism on its own level. This is the sentimental-aesthetic answer: what matter if all the facts are misconceived? The fancy (if you call it so) is beautiful in itself and touches emotions that we have a right to value. In your laboratory you may claim to have reduced the universe to a dust of atoms and the atoms themselves to electrical charges—but let us

> that are of purer fire
> Imitate the starry quire.

The sentimental reply is just as superficial as the brutal objection and more contemptible. Pythagoras himself would have expelled the aesthete from his community; but he would have entreated the man of science to tell him more about electrons and protons. He would never admit that the beauty he sought was the rainbow in a bubble destined to burst at the touch of the crudest fact. The advance of truth could not subvert the dominion of beauty. This was the core of his faith. To some minds it may still appear sentimental, charged with a warmth of feeling which the intellect, if really free, would dissipate.

Let us, then, consider the system of Pythagoras first under the aspect of truth. Curiously enough, on this side, where it seems weakest, the theory is most easily defended. If we look beneath the surface details, we find at the centre an intuition which has guided the whole course of mathematical physics from its founder Pythagoras to the present day: 'The nature of things is Number.' If the intellect would embrace the universe with the grasp of knowledge, it must subdue the unlimited welter of qualities, assailing our senses with a bewildering host of colours and sounds, to the principle of quantity; it must weigh and measure and count. The key to intelligible order lies in the notion of limited quantity defining unlimited quality, as the key to harmony lies in a few definite intervals marked out in the indefinite range of sound. This was a theoretical discovery comparable to the greatest of all man's practical inventions, the alphabet. It cost the labour of many generations and perhaps of several peoples to perfect that invention, which enabled us to convey in writing the unlimited world of spoken thought by the combinations of some twenty-four symbols. But it is to the individual genius of Pythagoras that science owes the clue which has ever since been followed by mathematical physicists—by Plato, by Leibniz and Newton, and by Einstein. So when the husk of his cosmology was shattered, the kernel survived.

I spoke of Pythagoras divining the principle of his philosophy by intuition, but there is a danger in the use of these psychological terms. They suggest that our minds are a bundle of distinct faculties working separately, like the band of warriors ensconced in the Trojan Horse, each peering out through his private loophole. When I speak of intuition, I by no means exclude intellect and feeling, or even sense-perception. The total state of our consciousness always contains all these elements. As the focus of attention shifts, it seems as if energy were gathered into some one of these elements at the expense of the rest. A reader absorbed in his book is unaware that his eyes are hard at work upon the lines of type, and his ear registering sounds that he does not hear. When his wife breaks in with a question, what the weather will be like to-morrow, he feels a wrench with a characteristic emotional revulsion, as he forces his attention to study the clouds and his intellect to weigh the chances of rain and sunshine. Meanwhile his train of thought drops into the penumbra of consciousness. What becomes of it, while he is patiently explaining that it is rash for an amateur to forecast the weather even for an hour? The train of thought is not blotted out of existence. Perhaps it remains in suspense; but possibly he may return to find that it has gone forward of its own momentum. This trivial experience may serve to illustrate the alternation of various phases of consciousness, and how they may all be kept in play, though the attention be engaged now in one quarter, now in another.

To return to Pythagoras' discovery: it is certain that a long travail must go before the birth of an intuition such as this, which suddenly sees widely scattered patches of knowledge as significant parts of a coherent picture. I suspect that, in approaching the moment of illumination, the soul must have reached out with every power intent; and moreover, that such phases of enhanced activity have alternated with other phases of passive acceptance, where thought was merged in feeling and strength was drawn from the humblest roots of being.

The final act of recognition must be overwhelming, because the truth, in such a moment of insight, is not presented as an intellectual formula, compact and comprehensible. It comes rather as an undefined mass of significance, fused in a glow of intense feeling. It may take years or generations for all the meaning and implications to be drawn out and expressed in words. In that process the glow of feeling fades out, and it may be forgotten that it was an essential part of the original experience. Certainly the apprehension of beauty—in particular, the beauty of harmonious sound—inspired the theory of Pythagoras, which could never have been framed by mere cool deductions of logical reasoning. The theory was born of the marriage of thought and feeling, in the fullness of an experience like that which I have imagined as felt in common by the man and woman, Lorenzo and Jessica. When the feeling has passed, the thought is left, an intellectual content distilled into the language of prose. The gold is now coined into a counter that can be passed from hand to hand. It may be depreciated or defaced, and become at last an idiot's plaything or a curiosity in an antiquary's cabinet.

So with this doctrine: 'All things are Number.' That is the barest extract; the words, just in themselves, mean little, and that little might be understood, while the feeling is neglected. The man of science, tracing from its source in that formula the main stream of mathematical physics, will be inclined to take the formula as preserving the only element of truth and value in Pythagoras' system, and to discard the harmony of the soul and of the spheres as so much dross. For the man of religion, on the other hand, the scientific statement will have no interest; he will find his profit in the recognition that the soul is immortal and may achieve perfection by becoming attuned to some divine principle in the universe. Pythagoras would say to both: What is your warrant for valuing one part of my experience and rejecting the rest? One of you will listen only to the head, and the other only to the heart. If I had done so, you would never have heard my name. It may be that nothing I taught is true in the letter: but if any part is true in the spirit, then the whole is true. Seek truth and beauty together; you will never find them apart. With the Angel of Truth your mind may wrestle, like Jacob: 'I will not let thee go except thou bless me'; but Beauty is the Angel of Annunciation, before whom the soul must be still as a handmaid: 'Be it unto me according to thy word.'

THE UNWRITTEN PHILOSOPHY[1]

IT would not be surprising if every lecture in this course should open with the same reflection; that the literature, the history, the philosophy, we have inherited from the ancient world bear much the same relation to the total product in those fields that the contents of the Ashmolean bear to the cities and temples, theatres and houses, that once formed the complete and familiar scene of ancient life. The most cherished exhibits in these galleries have been unearthed from ruins and waste-dumps and rubbish-heaps. Few are perfect; and the most perfect are often the least significant. The rest are fragments, which may or may not be susceptible of more or less dubious reconstruction.

In philosophy we are fortunate in possessing two great monuments of the highest significance, standing out in the centre of our field—the entire works of Plato, and a large body of Aristotle's more technical writings. Of the earlier, formative period all the surviving remains could be printed in a very slender volume. The only Presocratic document which extends to more than half its original size is the first part of Parmenides' poem—about 120 lines. The Milesian School is represented by two sentences and a few phrases. The fragments of Heracleitus, Empedocles, Anaxagoras, Democritus, are so disjointed that they cannot even be arranged in a probable order.

After Aristotle we have the letters of Epicurus, and then not a single writing by an original thinker of the first rank till we come to Plotinus. There is a much larger mass of fragments, but of greatly inferior value; because the succeeding eight centuries produced very few men worthy to stand beside that constellation of men of genius, the Presocratics. If the excavators of Herculaneum should bring to light the 750 books of Chrysippus—which Heaven forbid—any student would cheerfully exchange them for a single roll of Heracleitus.

[1] A lecture delivered to candidates for 'Greats' at Oxford.

Such being the state of the materials, a course of study in ancient philosophy is bound to concentrate attention on the works that exist in readable form—the works of Plato and Aristotle. But there are certain dangers in studying them in isolation from their context, and relying on handbooks for a bird's-eye view of the rest of the field. Our histories of philosophy have to eke out the scanty fragments by the testimony of ancient handbooks. These were uncritical compilations, based, at second or third or fourth hand, on the first history of philosophy, written by Aristotle's colleague Theophrastus. Theophrastus himself, though he knew the earlier philosophers at first hand, was apt to repeat statements about their doctrines which are to be found in Aristotle; and Aristotle was more interested in the construction of his own system than in the historical question, what his predecessors actually meant. He treated their speculations as imperfect forecasts of the truth he was engaged in discovering; and his testimony cannot safely be detached from its context and used as an uncoloured statement of fact. The result is that the whole doxographic tradition, derived from Theophrastus, is under suspicion of a Peripatetic bias, not to mention the inaccuracies and misunderstandings contributed by the later compilers.

These are some of the difficulties and dangers besetting the task of recovering what the ancient philosophers meant, even when we know what they actually said. My business is to consider whether there are any principles, over and above the application of common sense, to guide us in reconstructing what is lost, and interpreting what is extant.

Let us go back to the analogy with the reconstruction of material objects. If you confront an expert like Professor Beazley with a few broken potsherds, he will recreate from them a *krater* of Euphronius. In favourable cases, his fellow-experts will accept the result, within a narrow margin of error, because they will recognise that it is based on knowledge of two things: first, the individual style of Euphronius, and second, the whole tradition of structure and design, within which any work of Euphronius will fall into a definite place.

Now it is no less true that every system of philosophy has its individual style and its place in a historic tradition. Both things must be taken into account, whether we are trying to reconstruct the system from shattered fragments, or to interpret the expression of it in completely extant writings. In one obvious respect, we are at a serious disadvantage, as compared with the archaeologist. Every system of philosophy is unique. The archaeologist is guided by the analogy of a score of vases of the same pattern and similar design, some from the hand of the same master. But the historian of philosophy is not helped by so much as one parallel attempt to formulate the system of Heracleitus or Anaxagoras. The individual style has to be discovered from the fragmentary remains of a single example. Experience shows that we have, consequently, a much smaller chance of producing a result that will convince a fellow-expert.

Another point of difference is this. A material work of art, once restored to its original condition, speaks for itself. We can take it as the most complete expression that the artist's skill could achieve, of what he set out to express. There are no reservations—nothing that the artist could have any motive, conscious or unconscious, for keeping in the background or suppressing altogether. Philosophers, on the other hand, are less open and candid. We cannot always take what they say at its face value. Yet that is just what they would like us to do. Each system professes to be a structure of rational argument, which, if it is ever valid, claims to be valid for all minds at all times and places. It claims, in fact, to be like a system of geometry, based on premisses that seem to be intuitively certain, and deducing conclusions which everyone must accept as necessary consequences. The ancients, in particular, always had this ideal in mind, because geometry was then the only science with a developed technique, which assured a continuous and triumphant advance in discovery. The spectacle of this growing body of universally valid truth in mathematics encouraged the belief that there was one complete and coherent system, in which all truth about the world could be formulated. It encouraged also the corresponding belief that the human reason, whose work is to discover and know this truth, was not human, but divine—all our frailties, misunderstandings, ignorances, were traceable to its temporary association with the lower part of our nature, which reason finds it hard to dominate completely. If reason could once establish perfect authority, or perfect detachment from unruly passions and desires, then all our minds would see the one truth as it really is, and find themselves in absolute agreement. Meanwhile, each philosopher was inclined to credit his own reason with clear and unbiased vision, and to lay the blame for disagreement on the clouds that darkened the eyes of his neighbours. So each system was announced with dogmatic confidence as the revelation of dispassionate thought.

Even the science of nature was carried on with the least possible reference to observable fact. It was, indeed, concerned from the outset with facts that could never be observed, such as the origin of the world, before man existed. The intellect must assume that the world is intelligible; and that leads naturally to the further assumption that the processes of nature, and even the course of human history, must move on lines that our own reason might have laid down beforehand. If we flatter ourselves that the modern world has outgrown that delusion, let us remember that it is not so very long since Fichte taught that the philosophy of history 'has to correct our ideas of what seems on the evidence to have happened, by telling us what must have happened on the inherent "reasonableness" of its so happening.' Mr Carritt quotes Fichte's words:[1]

The philosopher must deduce from his adopted principles all possible phenomena of experience. But it is clear that, in the fulfilment of this purpose, he does not require the aid of experience; he proceeds purely as a philosopher, paying no respect whatever to experience; rather he describes time as a whole, in all its possible epochs, absolutely *a priori*.

And after Fichte, came Hegel; and after Hegel, Marx.

Nowadays there are still people who believe themselves to be in possession of the absolute truth about the most important matters; but no one of the creeds they accept is identical with any ancient Greek system. So we see those bygone systems now as facts of history, which occurred at a certain time and place, and could have occurred at no other, because they had certain causes

[1] E. F. Carritt, *Morals and Politics* (Oxford, 1935), p. 160.

that combined to produce them just there and then. We refuse to acknowledge their claim to be timeless, purely rational, universally valid. Yet perhaps we still treat them too much as they would like to be treated. There is a temptation to regard the history of philosophy as the record of a debate, carried on by a succession of speakers, each putting forward his own arguments and criticising the others. On the surface, there is much truth in this. A philosopher often does start from where his master left off; he modifies, improves, elaborates. Equally often he developes his opinions in opposition to other schools which he detests; or he replies to their criticism. As Aristotle remarks, 'We are all inclined to direct our inquiry, not by the matter itself, but by the views of our opponents; and even when interrogating oneself, one pushes the inquiry only to the point at which one can no longer put up any opposition.'[1]

But the history of philosophy ought not to resemble too closely the minute-book of a debating-society controlled by a competent chairman. If we dwell too much on these influences and interactions, it becomes fatally easy to weave the succession of systems into a neat pattern, preconceived by the historian, as if they were parts of a single design, supplementing and playing into one another. It is true that, less than a century after it began, ancient philosophy, in the hands of Parmenides and Heracleitus, became a controversy, and remained so to the end. None the less, at least throughout the creative period, from Thales to Aristotle, each system should be regarded as a self-contained work of art, with an inner life of its own, to which influences and reactions are secondary and subordinate. At the centre of the system is the source of its life, the philosopher himself, the spider who has spun the web. Or rather, perhaps, the philosopher, like the spider, prefers to conceal his person and leave the web with an innocent appearance of having spun itself. His motive is not modesty, but one that was ruthlessly exposed by William James—a man who saw the history of philosophy with the eye of a psychologist and a wisdom born of shrewd experience of human nature. Near the beginning of his book on pragmatism, James wrote as follows:

[1] *De Caelo* 294 B 7.

The history of philosophy is to a great extent that of a certain clash of human temperaments. Undignified as such a treatment may seem to some of my colleagues, I shall have to take account of this clash and explain a good many of the divergencies of philosophers by it.

Of whatever temperament a professional philosopher is, he tries, when philosophising, to sink the fact of his temperament. Temperament is no conventionally recognised reason; so he urges impersonal reasons only for his conclusions. Yet his temperament really gives him a stronger bias than any of his more strictly objective premisses. It loads the evidence for him one way or the other, making for a more sentimental or a more hard-hearted view of the universe, just as this fact or that principle would. He *trusts* his temperament. Wanting a universe that suits it, he believes in any representation of the universe that does suit it. He feels men of opposite temper to be out of key with the world's character, and in his heart considers them incompetent and 'not in it' in the philosophic business, even though they may far excel him in dialectical ability.

Yet in the forum he can make no claim, on the bare ground of his temperament, to superior discernment or authority. There arises thus a certain insincerity in our philosophic discussions: *the potentest of all our premisses is never mentioned.* I am sure it would contribute to clearness if we should break this rule and mention it, and I accordingly feel free to do so.

James goes on to characterise two main types of temperament— the tender-minded rationalist who goes by principles, and the tough-minded empiricist who goes by what he calls facts. The more recent theory of psychological types prefers the terms introvert and extrovert with various qualifications. The grouping of philosophers under these two main types can be traced all through. We think at once of Plato and Aristotle. Aristotle is the extrovert or empiricist pupil of an introvert and rationalistic master, constantly betraying the irritation due to the clash of temperament, struggling *not* to be a Platonist and to escape from the other world into the world of facts. Before them, there is the alignment of the Western mystical tradition over against the Ionian philosophy of nature; and later, again, the tender-minded Stoic confronts the tough-minded Epicurean.

The contrast has been plain enough, ever since Plato described it in the *Sophist* as the battle of Gods and Giants; but the conspiracy of silence, noted by James in philosophic debate, is still observed by historians of philosophy, who would perhaps feel that there was something not quite decent in the indiscretion of a breezy American. They are as disinclined as the philosophers themselves to lay bare temperamental motives behind the façade of rational argument. The materials for a genuine biography of Plato exist in his letters and in the indirect evidence of his dialogues. Wilamowitz, being a man of letters and not a professional teacher of philosophy, had the courage to make some use of them. One day, when psychology has become respectable, that life will be written by a man of genius, with no academic reputation to lose.

When a philosophy survives only in fragments, there is more excuse for a failure to grasp the character of its author. Yet, even so, the diversity of opinions about Heracleitus (for instance) is little short of scandalous. Heracleitus has been called a pantheist, a panzoist, and a panlogist; a sensualist and empiricist (by Schuster); a rationalist and idealist (by Lassalle); an optimist (by Pfleiderer) and a pessimist (by Mayer). He would not have understood most of these epithets; and the epithets he would have used in return would have been simpler, but not less impressive. We possess a fair number of his utterances which the ancients regarded as most characteristic, and some illuminating anecdotes. It ought not to be impossible to classify his temperament, and decide, with a reasonable certainty, that he could not have held some of the doctrines ascribed to him.

In the passage I quoted from William James the most significant remark, for our purpose, is this: 'The potentest of all our premises is never mentioned.' James is referring to the philosopher's unconscious syllogism: 'The world ought to satisfy my temperamental preferences: it will satisfy them, if it is like this: therefore it *is* like this; and my business is to find arguments to prove it, arguments that will appear purely reasonable and dispassionate.' This syllogism remains unconscious, because it is overlaid by that belief I mentioned—the belief that we possess a divine reason, animated by the desire for truth, and capable of detachment from all other desires and emotions. Now it is true that philosophers, at all times, have risen above personal ambitions and cupidities. Also, in the ancient world, when natural science was a part of philosophy, the study of nature had no connection with the exploitation of natural powers and resources for economic ends. In both these ways philosophy was *disinterested* and really detached from the importunities of daily life. On the other hand, no philosopher has ever succeeded in becoming completely superhuman or (if you prefer to put it so) completely *inhuman*. As Unamuno has said:[1]

In the starting-point of all philosophy—in the real starting-point (the practical, not the theoretical)—there is a wherefore. The philosopher philosophises for something more than the sake of philosophising. *Primum vivere, deinde philosophari*, says the old Latin adage; and as the philosopher is a man before he is a philosopher, he must needs live before he can philosophise, and in fact he philosophises in order to live.

A passage from Nietzsche[2] puts a finer point on this observation:

It has gradually become clear to me what every great philosophy up till now has consisted of—namely the confession of its originator, and a species of involuntary and unconscious autobiography; and, moreover, that the moral (or immoral) purpose in every philosophy has constituted the true vital germ out of which the entire plant has always grown. Indeed, to understand how the abstrusest metaphysical assertions of a philosopher have been reached, it is always well (and wise) to first ask oneself: What morality do they (or does he) aim at? Accordingly I do not believe that an 'impulse to knowledge' is the father of philosophy; but that another impulse, here as elsewhere, has only made use of knowledge (and mistaken knowledge!) as an instrument.

Here is a philosopher letting the psychological cat out of his own bag. I wonder if Nietzsche realised how completely this penetrating remark applied to himself.

Now, in Greek philosophy, throughout the eight and a half centuries from the death of Aristotle to the closing of the schools by Justinian, the truth pointed out by Nietzsche came visibly to

[1] *The Tragic Sense of Life* (trans. Flitch), p. 29.
[2] *Beyond Good and Evil* (trans. H. Zimmern), p. 10.

the surface. Everyone can see that, from the days of Zeno and Epicurus onwards, philosophy became essentially moral philosophy. Ethics, as we say, overshadowed and prejudiced logical speculations and the study of nature. The vital question was: What is the ultimate good in which human happiness can be found? And, looking beyond mankind to the world as a whole: Is the universe governed by a moral power, which has some care for man, or is it not? Stoic and Epicurean alike might take for their motto Augustine's words: 'Man has no motive to philosophise, save that he may be happy'—*Nulla est homini philosophandi causa, nisi ut beatus sit*—a saying which comes to very much the same thing as the passage just quoted from Nietzsche. Both the great systems are fortresses, built to shelter souls haunted by despair, and to make it possible to achieve resignation, self-mastery, and peace of mind.

So philosophy became frankly moral and anthropocentric. But it was already so, though less frankly and obviously, in the earlier creative period. Before Zeno and Epicurus, the question "How must we live in order to be happy?" had been brought into the foreground by Socrates. When Plato composed the *Phaedo*, he had come to see in this reorientation of philosophy the essential achievement of his master. Towards the end of the dialogue, he makes Socrates describe it as a sort of intellectual conversion that Socrates had experienced in his own person. But Plato knew that it was of much deeper significance than a passage in the biography of any individual; it was a crisis—perhaps the most important crisis—in the history of European philosophy. Socrates turned away from the old questions: What are things ultimately made of? How did the world we live in come to exist, as we see it, out of some primitive disorderly condition? The second half of Socrates' life had been spent in the atmosphere of a great war, in which the foundations of moral life were quaking, and traditional institutions were failing to save it from wreck. In such conditions a great mind, capable of preserving its detachment, may well come to declare that the end of man's life—what we should live for—is a more pressing problem than the beginnings of the physical world.

36

Accordingly, the philosophies that spring, directly or indirectly, from Socrates are at heart moral philosophies. For all his rationalism, Plato's thought constantly gravitates to the practical reform of society. So we put the matter, in abstract and impersonal terms. But there is something warmer and more human behind it. For what is Plato's remedy for the evils of his time? That 'the philosopher should be king'—again an abstract and impersonal statement. But in the Seventh Letter Plato has told how he arrived at it. During the last years of the war and for some time afterwards he had been pressed by his friends to enter public life. He had been tempted to yield on several occasions, but held back to watch their proceedings, before he would commit himself to joining them. Each time he had been revolted by an act of glaring injustice; and the conclusion was that there was no individual statesman or party with whom he could co-operate.

The result was [he writes] that I, who had at first been full of eagerness to take part in public life, when I saw all this happening and everything going to pieces, fell at last into bewilderment. I did not cease to think in what way all these things might be amended, and especially the whole organisation of the State; but I was all the while waiting for the right opportunity for action.

At last I saw that the constitution of all existing States is bad and their institutions all but past remedy, without a combination of radical measures and fortunate circumstance. I was driven to affirm, in praise of true philosophy, that only from the standpoint of such philosophy could one take a true view of public and private right; and that, accordingly, the race of man would never see the end of trouble until the genuine lovers of wisdom should come to hold political power, or the holders of political power should, by some divine appointment, become genuine lovers of wisdom.

The *Republic*, from beginning to end, explains and justifies this thesis. The genuine lover of wisdom—the philosopher—is the man whose character and intellect have been so trained that he has learnt the real difference between good and evil, the true value of all the ends that men pursue in life. Society is now governed, not by such men, but by the lovers of wealth and power, who cannot conceive a higher end for statesmanship than that their own country should be the richest and the strongest. Their own lives are ordered on the same principle. The question answered in the *Republic* is this: What are the least changes to be made in the Greek city-state, that will secure that these men who now rule shall be put in their proper place—a subordinate place—and the state shall be governed by men who know what really makes life worth living?

The city-state is a thing of the past; but essentially the same problem confronts modern society. One who has read the *Republic* will watch, as a tragic spectacle, the nations turning for salvation to dictators, who still believe that all will be well when all citizens are equally rich (or poor) or when their own country has more military power than any other.

Platonism can be regarded as essentially a demand for the reversal of current moral values, crystallised in this doctrine that mankind will never be happy until the lover of wisdom is king. It would be interesting to consider how far this doctrine is compatible with the modern panacea, which consists in turning society upside down with a view to obliterating all social distinctions; interesting—but irrelevant to our subject. The point to which I must return is that the moral impulse, detected by Nietzsche, is not the least of those 'potent premisses', which are not, indeed, altogether unmentioned, but which govern the direction, and predetermine the conclusions, of abstract thought more effectively than the thinkers themselves are aware. As I say, you could build the whole structure of Platonism round that central scheme for the reform of society. What we call the theory of Forms or Ideas, and the whole conception of the universe that goes with it, could be represented, not unfaithfully, as deducible from the moral thesis. And because we happen to possess a few of Plato's letters, we can see, behind that thesis, the emotional stress of the personal problem from which it took shape.

So far I have been speaking of the element of individual style, as one of the factors to be reckoned with in reconstructing a system from fragments, or interpreting a complete philosophical work. We must divine the philosopher's temperament as a means to deciding what he could, or could not, have taught, and, in many cases, we must look for a moral motive behind theories that seem, on the surface, to have little or no bearing on the conduct of human life.

Let us turn now to the other factor, the cultural tradition, which gives to ancient philosophy, as a whole, a character distinct from mediaeval or modern thought. This is a matter of intellectual climate—the atmosphere breathed in common by all members of a given civilisation, speaking the same language. We come here to premises and assumptions which are much less likely to be explicitly mentioned, precisely because they are the common property of all the philosophers, not points of difference such as emerge in controversy. No dispute can be carried on unless both parties have some fundamental standpoint on which they agree. This common basis is the last thing of which they are likely to be aware. Hence in the philosophic debate it is apt to pass almost wholly unmentioned.

I may here quote Dr Whitehead:

When you are criticising the philosophy of an epoch, do not chiefly direct your attention to those intellectual positions which its exponents feel it necessary explicitly to defend. There will be some fundamental assumptions which adherents of all the various systems within the epoch unconsciously presuppose.

Here is a plain warning that, if we would really understand what a philosopher says, we must keep a wakeful eye on what he does *not* say, because both he and his opponents take it for granted.

There are no personal motives for concealment here. The premises now in question are not mentioned simply because they seem too obvious to be worth mentioning. This brings us to the consideration of the current language in which the philosophies of any given age must be expressed. Philosophy requires an exceptionally large proportion of abstract words; and the discipline of translating into, and out of, Greek and Latin has taught us that abstract words—as distinct from the names of tangible objects—have a strange habit of shifting their meanings. This happens within the continuous life of the language itself, by a process which is imperceptible because it occurs in response to wholly unconscious needs. Take a word like *logos*. The Stoics borrowed the word, and much that it stood for, from Heracleitus; but no ancient Stoic could have told you how much meaning it had lost or gained in the two centuries between Heracleitus and Zeno. He would almost certainly assume that it meant to Heracleitus just what it meant to him. We may be sure that this is not true; but we, who think and write in English, have to contend with the further difficulty, that no modern word covers more than a fraction of the meaning that *logos* had for either Heracleitus or the Stoic. Modern philosophy is carried on mostly in terms that were translated from Greek into Latin, and then developed, along more or less diverging lines, in all the languages derived from Latin. Words are like coins. Shillings and half-crowns remain much the same in size and weight. Their constancy in appearance conceals from us the perpetual variations in their purchasing power. To realise that fully, we need a shock like the German period of inflation, when wages had to be paid twice a day because a pat of butter might cost a thousand marks in the morning, and two thousand in the evening. It is well to remind ourselves sometimes that everything written about ancient philosophy by modern scholars is, to a greater or less extent, vitiated and falsified by the linguistic exchange of currency, and by the underlying shift in the scope and content of concepts.

Even if we set aside the accidental difficulty of finding any modern equivalents for ancient words, there remains the problem dealt with by Ogden and Richards in their book called *The Meaning of Meaning*. When we speak of the meaning of a word, what is it, precisely, that we are talking about? This (as the readers of that book will know) is a very hard question to answer. All I can do is to offer a suggestion about the history of Greek philosophical terms.

The thought of the Greek race about the world—what it made of our natural environment—passed through two main stages: a magico-religious or mythical stage, and a philosophical or rational stage.

The mythical thinking of the earlier stage is partly rational: it offers explanations which satisfy an untrained and comparatively childlike intelligence. But the *form* of these explanations resembles day-dreaming—or dreaming proper—rather than the directed logical thinking which is governed by an effort of conscious attention, and uses language and abstract concepts. Dream-thought is a kind of *passive* thinking—the mind seems to watch a train of visual images, which pass before it unsummoned, as if arising spontaneously from some inner source. It is a flow of images and symbols, not of intellectual concepts or abstract ideas. In these concrete images and symbols, what we call the 'meaning' is enveloped in a wealth of sensuous content, which to the rational mind may seem, on analysis, to be irrelevant. The meaning, or thought, or idea, is immersed and disguised in symbols and pictures, and can be extracted only by a deliberate subsequent effort of analysis.

This description applies to speculation in the mythical stage. Take, as a simple instance, the notion of cosmogony—the becoming or beginning of existence of an ordered world. The abstract notion of *becoming* was still merged in the concrete image of *birth*: the words *genesis*, *gignesthai*, continue to be used for both.

In the mythical stage the accompaniments and associations of birth, and therefore of sex, are still involved in any becoming—the parents who are married, the father who begets, the mother who brings forth. So mythical accounts of the origin of the world take the form of a cosmo*gonia* or theo*gonia*. Each new factor is introduced as the offspring of a marriage. In Hesiod, for example, cosmogony is an indistinguishable part of theogony, and the whole evolution takes the form of a genealogical tree.

So the concrete image of birth is richer in content than the abstract idea of becoming (beginning to exist). But if we describe the extra content as 'associations', we must remember that at first it consisted of elements that had never been *dis*sociated. The abstract notion of becoming was only disengaged later, by eliminating the pictorial sex-imagery in the notion of birth.

This work of elimination and abstraction is not done all in a moment; it is a gradual process. The core of abstract meaning which rational thought is trying to isolate, remains surrounded by a penumbra of what will now be called 'associations'. These survive in poetry, because poets go on using concrete images in preference to prosaic concepts. Some of them the grammarian calls 'metaphors'; but a traditional metaphor is often not really the 'transference' of a word to a new sense. It may well be a fossilised association, holding together elements of thought that have become dissociated in the language of prose. After the primitive stage of genuine myth-making, there is a transitional period, in which the old images and symbols are retained, but with a nascent consciousness that they do go beyond the meaning proper.

In Hesiod himself they are on the way to becoming metaphor and allegory. When Hesiod speaks of the Muses as the daughters of Memory, that is not genuine myth. It is allegory—a thought that might be expressed in prose, but is more or less consciously disguised in language that is no longer meant literally. Pherecydes is a good example of the transitional phase. Aristotle mentions the old poets (*theologoi*) who made Zeus reign, not the first principle of things (Night, Chaos, Ocean). He then speaks of Pherecydes as belonging to a 'mixed class' who 'do not express themselves wholly in mythical terms'. The fragments of Pherecydes are in fact a mixture of myth, allegory, and literal statements.

Finally there may come a time when rational thinking consciously asserts itself, and the foremost intellects of the race awaken out of the dream of mythology. They perceive that the imagery of myth has become incredible and fantastic; and they demand literal, matter-of-fact truth. This happened in sixth-century Ionia, and what the Western world calls philosophy or science was born. The philosophers, trying to think clearly, discard the old representations. The aura of associations is dispelled, and the abstract concept—the tool of the new kind of thought—begins to emerge.

It is an easy fallacy (encouraged by dictionaries) to suppose that a word has at first a single sense—the sense that happens to be uppermost at its first occurrence in written records—and later accumulates other meanings. It is nearer the truth to say that the original meaning is a complex in which nearly all the later senses are inextricably confused. In etymology, if you dig down to the *root* of a word, you will often find that there have sprung from that same root a multitude of words whose meanings are now so completely dissociated that we cannot detect any connection between them. The elaboration of the concept is only the deliberate continuation, on the conscious level, of a branching process that has been going on unconsciously ever since man began to think and speak. Perhaps the greater part of it was already done before he began to write.

I suspect that, in an Oxford tutorial, one of the commonest questions is: 'What exactly do you mean when you say so-and-so?' The question is as old as Socrates and indeed dates from his time. We know that Socrates was interested in the lectures of Prodicus, the first man who tried to draw fine distinctions between so-called synonyms. But philosophic speculation had been going on for a good while before it was clearly realised that the most important terms were still ambiguous. It is characteristic of Aristotle that he solved many current problems by the discovery that this or that term has several senses. It was very hard for the Greek, who knew no language but his own, to find out that one word was doing duty for a number of concepts which could be distinguished by careful definition. In this way it happened that philosophic discussion, all the way through, rested on tacit assumptions, which were enshrined in the ambiguities of language. It was taken for granted that associations and connections of thought covered by a single word faithfully reproduced associations and connections between things—that the structure of the Greek language reflected the structure of the world. Plato himself wrote a whole dialogue (the *Cratylus*) to dispel the belief that every thing has a name which naturally belongs to it and embodies its real nature. So long as that was believed, it was inevitably assumed that all the associations of a word stood for real properties of the thing whose name it was.

Perhaps I can illustrate what I mean by taking two concepts which have long ago reached a very high degree of abstraction— the concepts of *Time* and *Space*. The whole framework of Time and Space, in which we spend our lives, has undergone no change in the last two thousand years; and until very recently it seemed obvious that the ancients must have conceived the properties of Time and Space as we do, or at least as we did, before we heard of the theory of relativity. For our purpose we may neglect that theory because it has not really penetrated the structure of our thoughts. Whatever mathematical physicists may say, we still imagine Time as a straight line reaching back without limit into the past and forward without limit into the future. And we imagine Space as a three-dimensional *continuum* of strictly unlimited extent. We cannot help believing that we could travel backwards or forwards in Time, and in any direction in Space, without ever retracing our steps or arriving at any end or beginning. That seems so clear that it may not occur to us to doubt whether it seemed equally clear to the ancient mind. But I think it can be shown that an ordinary Greek of, say, the fifth century would not have agreed with us. I believe it was just as obvious to him that Space was not an unlimited and shapeless extent, but finite and spherical; and that Time was not an endless straight line, but a circle. I cannot now produce the evidence for those conclusions. It is drawn partly from a study of the old associations bound up with the notion of Time and surviving in poetical imagery, partly from the explicit statements of the philosophers.

To take Space: it is true that in the fifth century the Atomists asserted the existence of a void, in which an unlimited number of material particles had unlimited room to move. But in so doing they were not formulating a view accepted by everyone as common sense. Before them Parmenides had declared that the whole of being is a finite sphere. Outside that sphere there can be neither *something* (for all being is inside) nor *nothing* (for nothing cannot exist). And after the Atomists, Plato and Aristotle are at one in teaching that the physical universe is spherical and finite, and in denying the existence of any empty space outside. If there is no empty space outside, the spherical universe of perceptible body must fill the whole of space. Space, therefore, is itself spherical and finite. The Epicureans—Lucretius for instance—continued to assert their unlimited void; but in the main the authority of Plato and Aristotle prevailed right on through the Middle Ages.

That Time was regarded as a circle is actually stated in so many words by Aristotle in the *Physics*. Time could not be dissociated from motion, and the motions by which time is measured are recurrent periods—the day, the month, the year—and the corresponding revolutions of the heavenly bodies. All these motions are circular. The attributes and associations of Time in poetry are manifestly borrowed from the cycle of the year, in which the life of nature moves from the death of winter to birth in spring, to maturity and decay, to death and rebirth—the cycle of becoming. If I may take these statements for granted without detailed proof, the point is that these abstract conceptions, which are for the most part tacitly assumed as the common property of a whole culture, entail religious and philosophical consequences of great importance.

With the assumption that Space is finite and spherical goes the belief that the earth which man inhabits stands at the centre of the universe, as Plato and Aristotle maintained. Aristarchus of Samos could not even succeed in giving the sun the central place, for all that the sun, as a divinity and the source of life and light, had long possessed an enormous prestige. There was immeasurably less chance for the impious Epicurean theory that our world as a whole—earth, planets and stars—was not at the centre of things, because there *is* no centre in infinite Space. The consequences are far-reaching. Dr Inge, among others, has remarked that the whole of Christian theology has never ceased to be geocentric. You may say that the vast profundities of space that have been revealed since Galileo made the first telescope have no real bearing on the value and importance of human life, in relation to the rest of the universe. It is none the less true that the whole of ancient and mediaeval cosmology and theology would have taken a very different shape, if an infinite Space, without centre or circumference, had been all along accepted as an obvious and unquestionable datum.

The circularity of Time also led to curious conclusions. It is not only in the Bible that man's history begins with a paradise lost and ends with a paradise regained. All ancient thought is haunted by regret for a golden age in the remote past and by the hope that the reign of Cronos will some day return. In the earliest philosophy it is assumed without question that the world had a birth in time, and will perish, to be succeeded by another. There is nothing whatever in the appearances of Nature to suggest such a daring theory. It is the primitive assumption of all cosmogony combined with the image of Time as a circle, in which the end is knit to the beginning. In Pythagoreanism appears the more precise doctrine of eternal recurrence: everything that happens now has happened before and will happen again for ever. The modern belief in a continuous progress of mankind from a brutish condition was stated, but could not establish itself in antiquity. Perhaps most people continued to hold, with Hesiod, that man had degenerated ever since the golden age. Plato naturally speaks of the rule of the philosopher, Virgil speaks of the reign of Augustus, as a return to the lost happiness of the past: *redeunt Saturnia regna*.

These cases illustrate the way in which not only physical and metaphysical theories, but the whole view of the course of human history, are governed by abstract schemes of conception that escape notice, because they so seldom need to be actually mentioned.

PLATO'S COMMONWEALTH[1]

A COUNTRY so situated that its growth depends on sea-power and foreign trade heads an alliance against an emperor bent on adding a good part of Europe to his dominions. The emperor is defeated; and in an ample stretch of comparatively quiet years the champion of freedom finds opportunity to take the lead among its neighbours in the arts of peace. At home, democratic institutions are developed towards their logical completion; abroad, ambition is satisfied by consolidating an empire overseas. A golden age of prosperity and progress—or so it will seem when men look back upon it from the darker days that are to come. For an expanding prosperity has to reckon with the jealousy of commercial rivals; and an expanding empire is not always welcomed as a boon by the countries it penetrates and absorbs. There is a growing tension. A continental power, whose citizens are trained to the highest pitch of military efficiency, declares war. The states are grouped in two alliances, neither of which is strong enough to overpower the other or to inflict a fatal wound. No soldier of genius appears on either side, and the war drags on in a series of futile successes and futile defeats. The strain of anxiety and the release of those ugliest passions which, in time of war, assume the name of virtue, demoralise the combatants. The tacit conventions that lie at the base of civilised life are called in question or openly denied. Men lose faith in democracy, and even in freedom; they come near to losing faith in life itself. Somewhere at the heart of their being a nerve snaps; and when the war of exhaustion comes to a disastrous close, they are left disheartened and listless, unable to believe in a future worth the effort they lack the driving-power to make.

That description (as perhaps you have guessed) was designed to leave you in doubt whether I was speaking of the history of Athens, from the struggle with Persia, through the golden age of

---

[1] The Samuel Dill Memorial Lecture, delivered at the Queen's University, Belfast, 1933.

Pericles, to the Peloponnesian War and the early manhood of Plato, or of the history of England, from the struggle with Napoleon, through the golden age of Victoria, to the war of 1914 and the early manhood of the younger generation.

Perhaps you do not believe (as the ancients believed) that human affairs move in cycles and that history repeats itself. But the men of my Victorian generation, to whom the war came in middle life, are struck by two features which seem common to the opening of the fourth century at Athens and the present time in England. One is the collapse—whether it be temporary or permanent—of the belief in democracy. The other is what looks to us Victorians like a failure of nerve in the generation to whom the war came in their childhood. Perhaps both features are symptoms of the same trouble. To believe in democracy you must believe in the essential goodness of common humanity, and it is hard to keep that faith when you have seen humanity at war. And if men lose faith in one another, perhaps they must also lose faith in themselves. Despairing of freedom, they may seek refuge in authority; despairing of persuasion, they may pin their hopes on violence. One after another, we have seen countries with more or less democratic institutions submit to dictators. Some individuals who feel their hand too weak to steer their own boat, or do not know whither to steer it, climb on board the great vessel of the Roman Church—not a democratic institution, but a hierarchy securely dependent on the infallible wisdom at its head. Others have found a wisdom no less infallible in an economic interpretation of history, teaching them how to become the tools of inexorable destiny.

In fourth-century Greece we can see something analogous to this longing for a political or spiritual dictatorship, to relieve ordinary men of a responsibility they cannot face, and guide their lives to some goal they cannot choose for themselves. Some of Xenophon's works show a hankering after benevolent despotism. His political romance, the *Cyropaedia*, transfigures the autocrat of Persia into a paternal monarch. He even found a living exemplar in Agesilaus, who ruled Greece for some six years. Antisthenes seems to have made Heracles into an ideal mythical king, enduring his labours for the good of mankind. Finally there is Isocrates.

Debarred from public life by a weak voice and impoverished by the war, Isocrates had set up a school where he taught young men looking forward to a public career to take a large view of international affairs and to reproduce the style of his own pamphlets with a scrupulous avoidance of hiatus. He looked to a nation on the northern fringe of the Greek world, a comparatively young nation, which had not been ground in the mill of the Peloponnesian War, and was, in the eyes of Hellenic purists, hardly to be counted as civilised. Isocrates saw the saviour of society in Philip of Macedon. Philip was, indeed, a man who knew his own mind. He created the military machine which enabled his son, Alexander, to turn the tables on Persia; prepared for him the path to the East by political manoeuvres; and in his diplomatic relations with the states that had once been leaders of Hellas, was capable of twisting their representatives round his little finger. Set beside Philip, Demosthenes, nursing his pathetic dream of restoring Athens to the place she had held under Pericles, seems as blind and futile as the European politicians of to-day.

For here the parallel I drew at the outset seems relevant again. The heads of the European states are still immersed in the old local feuds and jealousies, plotting for the hegemony of Europe; and all the while, on the eastern fringe, a young and semi-barbarous nation, under the iron hand of men who know their own minds and have a plan, is being taught to worship mechanical efficiency and to husband strength that might be used in an idealistic crusade. The modern counterparts of Demosthenes have no better means of meeting this situation than Demosthenes' weapons against Philip—ostracism and invective. But I will not push my parallel into the region of prophecy. We had better return to Athens.

Plato was born in 427 B.C., the year of the revolt of Mitylene and the revolution at Corcyra. In that year Cleon, urging the Athenians not to revoke their savage sentence to massacre the citizens of Mitylene and to enslave their women and children, had warned Athens that a democracy cannot govern an empire, that their rule was a despotism over unwilling subjects held down by force, that the three greatest enemies of their power were pity and eloquent sentiments and the generosity of strength, and that if, right or wrong, they were resolved to rule, then, rightly or wrongly, they must chastise the rebels for their good: otherwise, let them resign their empire, and, when virtue was no longer dangerous, be as virtuous as they pleased. At Corcyra the brutal massacre of the oligarchic party by the democrats drew from Thucydides his famous reflections on the demoralisation of character produced by war and revolution. It is here that he sets down the terrible truth:

In peace and prosperity both states and individuals are actuated by higher motives because they do not fall under the dominion of imperious necessities; but war, which takes away the comfortable provision of daily life, is a hard master and assimilates men's characters to their conditions.

This was not an auspicious year for the birth of a man whose distinguished family and extraordinary gifts should have marked him out for a brilliant part in the public life of Athens. The disaster of the Sicilian expedition came when Plato was fourteen; the fall of Athens when he was twenty-three. The democracy was then restored; but not the old faith in democracy. A few years later Socrates was condemned to death. This event soon gathered a symbolic significance never foreseen by the authors of the charge: 'Socrates is guilty of not recognising the gods whom the State recognises.' In the sense intended the charge was false; but in a deeper sense it was true enough. Henceforth the wise man was to go his own way, following gods whom no State has ever recognised.

If we possessed only the shorter dialogues which Plato wrote in the dozen years after the death of Socrates, we should have very little clue to his state of mind. He set himself to think out, for his own guidance and for the enlightenment of his fellow-citizens who had condemned Socrates, the essential significance of his master's thought, which was not easy to grasp. He chose to write in the form of dramatic dialogues, with the scene laid far back in the days of his own childhood, or even before his birth. No troubles and misgivings of his own were allowed to darken the atmosphere of these pictures of a bygone generation. We could not guess at the passions working under this serene surface were it not for the *Gorgias*, a longer dialogue which falls at the end of this first period, and a passage in the Seventh Letter. This letter was written, near the end of Plato's life, to the surviving friends of Dion at Syracuse, when Dion's death had finally eclipsed all the hopes that inspired Plato's excursions to Sicily.

When I was young [he means in the early twenties] I had the same experience that comes to so many: I thought that as soon as I should be my own master, I should enter public life. This intention was favoured by certain circumstances in the political situation at Athens. The existing constitution was generally condemned, and a revolution took place. [This was the revolution of the Thirty Tyrants in 404.] ...Some of the leaders were relatives and friends of mine, and they at once invited me to co-operate, as if this were the natural course for me to take. My feelings were such as might be expected in a young man: I imagined that they would bring the State, under their management, from an iniquitous to a right way of life. Accordingly I watched closely to see what they would do.

It was not long before I saw these men make the earlier constitution seem like a paradise. In particular, they sent Socrates, my friend, then advanced in years—a man whom I should not hesitate to call the most righteous man then living—they sent Socrates with other persons to one of the citizens with instructions to arrest him by violence for execution. Their purpose, no doubt, was to involve Socrates, with or without his consent, in their proceedings. Socrates refused, preferring to face any danger rather than be a party to their infamous acts. Seeing all this and other things as bad, I was disgusted and drew back from the evils of the time.

Not long afterwards the Thirty fell, and the whole constitution was changed. Once more I was attracted, though less eagerly, by the desire to take part in political action. In those unquiet times much was still going on that might move one to disgust, and it was no wonder that, during the revolutionary changes, some took savage vengeance upon their enemies; but on the whole the returning exiles showed great moderation. Unfortunately, however, some of the men in power brought my friend Socrates to trial on an infamous charge—the very last that could be made against Socrates—the charge of impiety. He was condemned and put to death—he who had refused to have any hand in arresting one of the accusers' own friends when they themselves were in exile and misfortune.

51

When I considered this and the men who were directing public affairs, and made a closer study, as I grew older, of law and custom, the harder it seemed to me to govern a State rightly. Without friends and trustworthy associates it was impossible to act; and these it was not easy to find among my acquaintance, now that Athens was no longer ruled by the manners and institutions of our fathers; nor was it possible to make new associates with any ease. At the same time the whole fabric of law and custom was going from bad to worse at an alarming rate. The result was that I, who had at first been full of eagerness to take part in public life, when I saw all this happening and everything going to pieces, fell at last into bewilderment. I did not cease to think in what way all these things might be amended, and especially the whole organisation of the State; but I was all the while waiting for the right opportunity for action.

In such a situation it would be harsh to accuse Plato of failure of nerve. But the whole of this long letter reveals—what we might guess from his other writings—that his powers and gifts were of such a kind that he could never be a leading man of action in the society of his time. The plane on which his mind habitually moved was not one from which he could make effective contact with the plane of political life in a demoralised society. By the man of action I mean the type of man who sees that, if he is to get anything done, he must ally himself with associates who are not altogether to his mind, lay aside ideal aspirations for some future day that will never come, and condescend to opportunism and compromise. But Plato is already dreaming of an ideal organisation of society. He even imagines that the Thirty Tyrants (of all men) might effect a moral reformation. He transfers his hopes to the restored democracy, only to find them shattered once more. And all the time he is thinking and waiting for the right moment to act. It is not surprising that the right moment never came.

Meanwhile, he writes the early dialogues, thinking out Socrates' philosophy of life and finding it to be a philosophy that stands in uncompromising conflict with all the current ambitions and aims of the practical man of the world. That conflict is brought upon the stage and fought out to the end in the last part of the *Gorgias*. The antagonists are Socrates and Callicles. Socrates is the man of thought, who had studiously kept clear of politics and thereby avoided the fate that was to overtake him in old age. Callicles is not an historical character. He is the ideal representative of the man of the world—a young man looking forward, like Plato himself, to a career of statesmanship, and armed for it with a very different view of life, which he states at length and with astonishing force. He believes in the natural right of the strong man to rule the weak and take to himself the lion's share of all worldly advantages. The conventional idea that such self-assertion is unjust he regards as put about by the weak and inferior, who cannot hope to assert themselves and so praise equality—the watchword of democracy. He has no patience with the cant about self-restraint and moderation. He professes to believe that happiness is to be found in indulging every natural appetite to the full. Socrates attacks this position with equal or greater force. He tells Callicles that this life of selfish ambition, seeking the satisfaction of every desire as it arises, is 'an unending round of evils, the life of a robber and an outlaw, who can never be the friend of man or the friend of God'. Callicles is not convinced. He shrugs his shoulders, leaving Socrates to point out that every statesman Athens has ever had is condemned by the standard he has set up. Socrates declares himself to be the only true statesman; but, if he were to take Callicles' advice and enter public life without surrendering his own ideals, he would certainly be put to death.

The choice between a political career and the philosophic life was not a choice that the real Socrates had ever had to face. Plato is thinking here of his own problem. The *Gorgias* is his final answer to the friends who had pressed him to join them, and perhaps also to the impulse within himself which had tempted him to yield. Callicles is the devil's advocate. Socrates' forecast of his own death is echoed by a later passage in that letter I have already quoted. In the course of some general reflections on the giving of political advice, Plato there says how the prudent man should deal with his city.

If he thinks the constitution is bad, he should say so, unless he sees that to say so will be useless or will bring about his own death. He must not have recourse to revolutionary violence. If that is the only possible expedient, he must refrain from action and pray for the best, both for himself and for his country.

That is the course finally taken by Plato himself. The long and painful period of indecision ended in the conclusion that he could never take part in the politics of a democratic state. And on this question he never changed his mind. In his retreat at the Academy he appears to us as completely detached from all that went on in the Assembly and the market-place as if the garden of the Academy had been the garden of Epicurus.

Callicles, in his spirited exhortation to Socrates to give up philosophy and play a man's part in active life, quotes, from the *Antiope* of Euripides, a famous debate between the Theban brothers, Zethus and Amphion, on this same contrast. Zethus urges Amphion, who had 'built the walls of Thebes with ravishing sound of his melodious lute', to give up the effeminate and unprofitable service of the Muse and take to agriculture, war, and politics. It is significant that this contrast between the active life and the contemplative should occur in a play of Euripides. Long ago, in the sixth century, the wise man had been the man of affairs, like Solon the lawgiver and others of the Seven Sages. The death of Pericles and the Peloponnesian War mark the moment when the men of thought and the men of action began to take different paths, destined to diverge more and more widely till the Stoic sage ceased to be a citizen of his own country and became a citizen of the universe. Pericles had been the last philosophic statesman. Socrates remarks in the *Phaedrus* that his loftiness of spirit was due to his converse with Anaxagoras, whose speculations about Nature and the intelligence that works in Nature had given Pericles an insight and breadth of view that he carried into his work as leader of the Assembly. After Pericles the men of thought, like Thucydides and Euripides, go into exile, voluntary or enforced. Socrates just fulfils his civic duties, but obeys the warning of his divine sign to keep out of politics. The task of winning, or losing, the war was left to business men like Cleon, or ambitious egoists like Alcibiades. When the war was over, there was not a man in public life with whom Plato could bring himself to co-operate.

And yet, in Plato's eyes, this drifting apart of the men of thought and the men of action was a disastrous calamity—indeed, the root of the social evils of his time. His problem, as presented in the *Gorgias*, could not be solved simply by dropping all interest in the fate of society and becoming absorbed in abstract speculations. Philosophy meant to him what it had meant to Socrates—not the contemplative study of science or metaphysics, but the pursuit of wisdom, which is the same thing as human perfection and happiness. And man is a social creature; the individual cannot gain perfection and happiness by living for himself alone. There are parts of his nature that can find scope only in the life of society. Hence philosophy and active citizenship were not—or ought not to be—two alternative careers. They should be combined in a single life; and the only perfect solution was to reunite the two elements that had been drifting apart. This is the conclusion which Plato, in that letter I quoted, tells us he had reached before he first went to Sicily, in or about his fortieth year. The passage I read continues as follows:

At last I saw that the constitution of all existing States is bad and their institutions all but past remedy, without a combination of radical measures and fortunate circumstance. I was driven to affirm, in praise of true philosophy, that only from the standpoint of such philosophy could one take a true view of public and private right; and that, accordingly, the race of man would never see the end of trouble until the genuine lovers of wisdom should come to hold political power, or the holders of political power should, by some divine appointment, become genuine lovers of wisdom. It was in this mind that I first went to Italy and Sicily.

This visit to western Greece was probably due to a desire to make acquaintance with the Pythagorean communities of lower Italy. Unexpectedly it led Plato to form hopes that the rule of a philosophic prince might actually be established. At Tarentum he formed a lifelong friendship with Archytas, who was both a mathematician of great distinction and a man who, at the head of

the government, had conducted successful wars against neigh-
bouring states. In Sicily the strong man at this time was the elder
Dionysius, the Machiavellian tyrant of Syracuse who had already
become master of nearly all Sicily and was now scheming
to add southern Italy to his dominions. Plato certainly never
dreamed of converting the elder Dionysius to philosophy; but
there is a passage in the *Republic* which may reflect hopes founded
on his son, Dionysius the younger, who was less than ten years old
at the time of Plato's visit.

No one will deny [says Socrates] that some prince might be born
with the philosophic nature, and that nature might escape corruption.
If only one such should arise, in control of a city which would obey
him, he might achieve all these things which now seem incredible—

the foundation of the ideal State.

Or these hopes might have been founded on Dion, another
lifelong friend made on this occasion. Dion, as the elder Dionysius' brother-in-law, held a position of influence at the Syracusan
Court. In the same letter Plato writes:

I became acquainted with Dion, then a young man, and without
knowing it began to work for the overthrow of a tyranny by telling
Dion what I thought was best for mankind and advising him to act
upon it. He, with ready understanding, was quick to grasp my arguments. He listened with keener attention than any young man I have
ever met; and he determined to live for the future a different life from
that of the Italians and Sicilians, preferring goodness to pleasure and
luxury. So he continued until the death of Dionysius, earning thereby
the dislike of those who led the usual life of a tyrant's courtiers.

Twenty years later, when the younger Dionysius succeeded his
father, Dion persuaded Plato to visit Syracuse again, and attempt
to carry his ideals into practice by training the young tyrant in the
principles of the *Republic*. Plato consented, with much doubt and
reluctance. But, though the younger Dionysius had shown some
promise of what Plato calls the philosophic nature, that nature had
not, in his case, escaped corruption. Also he was vain and con-
ceited. To persuade a young man already in possession of despotic
power, bequeathed by an ambitious and unscrupulous father, that

he must qualify himself for his position by a long training in pure mathematics was a task that few men would have attempted. It soon ended—as Plato in his heart must have known it would—in a fiasco. The philosopher had put himself into a false position, which any man of the world would have seen to be ridiculous, because he feared, more than ridicule, the reproach of being an idle dreamer who would not take an opportunity to carry his ideals into practice.

There remained another means of indirectly influencing practical life. This was to found a school of philosophic statesmen—to attract from foreign states young men whose position and prospects were more fortunate than those of Plato's own youth, and to give them such a training as would fit them for the art of statesmanship, as Plato conceived it. On his return from his first visit to Sicily, Plato founded the Academy. His own task was to direct this school in personal contact with his students. At the same time he continued to write Socratic discourses, setting forth his principles in a form that would reach the educated public all over the Greek world. Such writings would have the double advantage of making the Socratic philosophy known, and of attracting students to the Academy. Chief among the dialogues of this group is the *Republic*.

I cannot attempt, in so short a time, even the barest outline of what the *Republic* contains. But if there is any truth in the parallel I drew between the state of society in Plato's time and in our own, there is some interest in comparing his remedy for human troubles with the remedies held out to us. I do not mean the momentary expedients of bewildered politicians. I am thinking rather of more speculative schemes for the future of society. In the main, these schemes appear to have two aims in view. The first is to standardise mankind, by redistributing wealth so as to level down the distinction between rich and poor. The second is to raise the standard slightly by increasing the efficiency of the machines which are to do the hard work for us. We are then to enjoy a moderate degree of bodily comfort, and have leisure to frequent the cinema, read the Hundred Best Books, and do all the other things we should do if only we had time. In the last hundred years civilised man has fallen under the dominion of the machine, which has come, not only to regulate his life, but to permeate his imagination and his ideals. We are not yet at the end of this stage. For the present our dream of the future centres in the machine. As our machinery becomes more and more automatic, we shall be able to escape from minding it for a larger number of hours in the day.

And with the supremacy of the machine there arises the ideal of *order*, which (as Professor Zimmern has remarked) we are substituting for the ideal of personal freedom, associated with democracy. There is no place more orderly than a factory, no place where personal eccentricities are less welcome. But if we are destined to model the whole of life on factory life, the question who is to manage the factory will become urgent; and about that we seem to be rather vague. Do we want to be ruled by dictators, or by a directorate of Marxian doctrinaires, or by a conspiracy of business men? We are like a firm advertising for a manager with no clear notion of the qualifications required, and not much liking the looks of any of the applicants.

Now Plato too, as we have seen, had lost the belief in liberty, if liberty was to mean that every man should do as he pleased, and in equality, if equality was to mean that any citizen was just as fit as any other to hold office in the State; and he thought that democracy at Athens had come to rest on those principles. He too desired to substitute the ideal of order; and the problem of the *Republic* is to discover a type of social order that shall be stable and harmonious. Not living in a mechanical age, he did not look for a model to the factory with its despotic manager or its board of directors. The principle that guided him was this. A social order cannot be stable and harmonious unless it reflects the unalterable constitution of human nature. More precisely, it must provide a frame within which the normal desires of any human being can find legitimate scope and satisfaction. A social system which starves or thwarts any important group of normal human desires will, sooner or later, be overthrown by the forces it has repressed, and, while it lasts, will warp and pervert them.

It is at this point, I believe, that Plato's thought takes a different direction from the philosophy of his master, Socrates. There are two ways in which a man may approach the task of conceiving an ideal society. One is to start with the moral reformation of the individual, and then to imagine a society consisting of perfect individuals. That is the logical outcome of Socrates' mission to his fellow-citizens as described in the *Apology*. The other is to take individual human nature as we find it, and to construct a social order that will make the best of it as it is and as it seems likely to remain. This is the course taken by Plato in the *Republic*.

Let us consider for a moment Socrates' view of human nature. Socrates believed that in every human soul there is a faculty of insight, which, if once it could be cleared from the mists of prejudice and the illusions of pleasure which seems good when it is not, is capable of discerning where its own true happiness is to be found. The only thing in the world that is really and intrinsically good for man is the perfection of his own nature. All the other aims that we pursue—wealth and the pleasures it can buy, power and distinction, even bodily health—are in themselves valueless. To sacrifice any or all of them in the pursuit of perfection is really no sacrifice at all. We are only sacrificing what men call pleasure to gain happiness. Now, no one will believe this truth until he can see it for himself with the inward eye of his own soul; you cannot persuade him to act as if it were true until he knows it, with entire conviction, from his own experience. When he does know it in this complete sense, then he will act upon it unfailingly; his knowledge must determine his will, for no man will sacrifice his true happiness for pleasures he can see to be illusory. This knowledge is wisdom; and the man who gains it becomes thenceforth morally autonomous: everything he does is determined by his own inward light; he will not be guided by any external authority, but will claim the unconditional freedom of self-rule. Socrates did not concern himself directly with the reform of society. His mission was addressed to any individual who would listen to him. He spent his life trying to make individual men see for themselves the truth which he had seen, but could not teach them; for wisdom cannot be taught, or communicated by persuasion, or imposed by authority.

Now if we imagine this mission successfully accomplished, the reform of society would follow. The outcome would be a group of individuals, each one of whom would be completely self-ruled and free. Not only would each man enjoy inward harmony (the conflict of desires within his own soul having been finally reconciled), but also there would be no conflict or competition between one individual and the rest. If any set of men could be finally convinced that the perfection of the human soul is the only object of any value in itself, the clash of competing egoisms would disappear. No one man's gain would be another's loss. Such a society would need no laws. There would be no distinction of ruler and subject, for each man would govern himself. There would be perfect equality and unlimited freedom. The name for such a state of society is Anarchy, or (if you think of the ruling faculty of insight as divine) Theocracy. The men who condemned Socrates for not recognising the gods whom Athens recognised, and for turning the minds of young men against traditional authority, were dimly aware that Socrates' mission pointed to a subversion of all existing institutions.

But it was left to the Stoics to follow up the consequences into the political field. From the Socratic premiss that human perfection is the only thing of real value, and that this virtue is wisdom, they deduced the ideal of the perfect sage, who alone is self-sufficient, happy, and free. To him all things that he can desire are lawful. So we find Zeno, the founder of Stoicism, rejecting, in theory, all existing forms of constitution. The wise man can only be a citizen of the universe. There is no such thing as the ideal State on earth. If men were perfect, they would all be members of the City of Zeus.

It is significant that Zeno is known to have criticised Plato's *Republic*, because it is not the City of Zeus. Plato, it is true, has his scheme for the production of the perfect man, deduced from the same Socratic principles, combined with his own conception of all that knowledge or wisdom implies. But he does not say: First make every individual perfect, and then you will need no laws or civic institutions. He is too much bent upon the reform of Greek society to be ready to postpone it to the millennium. So he turns to the other possible course: taking human nature as it is, and making the best of it. Plato's commonwealth is not the City of Zeus or the Kingdom of Heaven. It is a reformed Greek city-state, surrounded by other city-states and by the outer world of barbarians, against which it may have to hold its own. Hence he does not contemplate the abolition of war, which figures in all modern Utopias. The problem he proposes for solution is: What are the least changes to be made in the highest existing form of society—the Greek city-state—which will put an end to intestine strife and faction, and harmonise the competing desires of human nature in a stable order?

Looking, then, to human nature as it is, Plato points to a given natural fact that any practical scheme must reckon with, namely, that men are not born all alike, but with temperamental differences sufficiently marked to group them in various types. It is not the business of education to smooth out these differences and level everyone up or down to the same pattern. Education should develope each type to the fullest life of which it is capable; and the social framework should provide a place in which that type can make its contribution to the life of the whole community, without sacrificing the fulfilment of its own characteristic desires.

First, then, we need a broad classification of human types, based on their dominant desires or motives. Now there was an old parable comparing human life to the Olympic festival, and dividing the people who went to such a festival into three classes, according to the motives which took them there. To some it was a fair or market, where they could buy and sell; their motive was gain. The competitors in the games went with a different purpose, to win honour and fame; their motive was a not ignoble ambition, or more generally the love of victory and power. Finally, there were the spectators, who sought neither gain nor honours, but went to contemplate a scene which must have been more attractive to Greek eyes than a football match in the Wembley Stadium. The three classes of visitors correspond to the three classes in Plato's State. These are not hereditary castes, but strata of society into which the citizens of each new generation are to be sorted out, solely on the ground of their natural temperament and abilities. First there is the money-making type—the lovers of wealth and of the pleasures that wealth can buy. Second, the lovers of honour and power, who desire distinction in the active life. Third, the men whom Plato calls philosophers, the lovers of wisdom and knowledge, the spectators of all time and all existence—a phrase that recalls an anecdote about Pericles' friend Anaxagoras. When Anaxagoras was asked what he thought made life worth living, he replied: 'The study of the heavens and of the whole order of the world.'

Now, if it be true that men can be roughly grouped according to these temperamental varieties of dominant motive, and if society can avail itself of this natural fact, then there is a possibility of these divergent types pursuing each its own satisfaction, side by side, without competition and conflict. This is the key to Plato's solution of the social problem. He does not propose to convert all his citizens to the ideal of any one type, but rather to draft the individuals of each type, as soon as their dispositions can be ascertained, into their proper place, and to secure that they shall stay there and discharge their function. To him it seemed that what was wrong with existing society was that these types do not keep in their places. The acquisitive and the ambitious types are always trying—and trying successfully—to control the life of the State and to direct its action to the ends they value. Hence society is governed by men who cannot conceive of any higher aim than to make their own country the richest and the most powerful. Unfortunately, wealth and power are what Aristotle calls 'goods that can be fought for'; neither the individual nor the State can indulge an unlimited desire for either except at the expense of others. The only remedy that Plato could see was to transfer supreme political power to the third type. The object of their desire is not a competitive object. If a man gains wisdom, it is not at his neighbour's expense. On the contrary, the more wisdom he can gain, the better it will be for them, if they can take advantage of it. The advantage they should take is to constrain him— reluctant though he may be—to take control of the State. So we reach the central proposition of the *Republic*:

Unless [says Socrates] either the lovers of wisdom become kings in their cities, or those who are now called kings and potentates come to love wisdom in the true sense and in sufficient measure—unless, in fact, political power and the pursuit of wisdom be united in the same persons, while the many natures which now take their several ways in one or the other direction are forcibly debarred from pursuing either separately, there can be no rest from troubles for the race of mankind, nor can this commonwealth that we have constructed in discourse ever, till then, grow into a possibility or see the light of day.

Who are these lovers of wisdom—philosophers—that they should rule over us? If the word 'philosopher' calls up before your mind an old gentleman with a long beard, bending over his study-table as he composes an article on some intricate problem of metaphysics, then you are in much the same position as Adeimantus in the *Republic*, who objects that specialists in philosophy, for the most part, become decidedly queer, not to say rotten, and even the better sort are entirely useless to their country. And you will find that Socrates assents to that objection. We must banish that picture of the philosopher from our imaginations. To Plato wisdom means, ultimately, what it had meant to Socrates—not only a knowledge of scientific or metaphysical truth but, above all, the knowledge of good and evil, the knowledge (as we say) of values. To possess wisdom is to know what is really good and worth living for; and that is the secret of happiness. It is true, Plato thought that such wisdom could be attained only by a small number of men, after an arduous intellectual training; but the claim of the philosopher to rule is based on his power to think clearly and the insight enabling him to assess the value of all objects of desire—to see that neither wealth nor power is the right aim either for the State or for the individual.

The institutions of Plato's commonwealth follow from the principles I have outlined. The principle that normal desires should be given a legitimate satisfaction dictates his solution of the problem that bulks so large in schemes of social reform—the redistribution of wealth. It excludes the idea, popular with some modern reformers, that wealth should be evenly distributed over the whole of society—a proposal commonly advanced by men who are not of the money-loving type, and contemplated without enthusiasm by the mass of mankind, even in Russia. Plato would make over all material property to the acquisitive type—the lovers of money—who are to form the third and lowest class, the industrials. They desire wealth, and they shall have it. In the enjoyment of a moderate amount of property—for extremes of poverty and of wealth must be prohibited—they shall find the reward of fulfilling their social function, which is to supply the economic needs of the whole commonwealth. He will thus set this type to the kind of work it likes and is fitted for—necessary and useful work—and make it contented by allowing it the rewards it understands and desires.

But this class must not govern, and we must make sure that it shall not want to govern. This is to be done by making the possession of property incompatible by law with the possession of authority in the State. So long as political power can be combined with wealth, and either can be made a means to the other, the business man will leave his counting-house and try to grip the levers of the political machine. The only way to prevent that is to effect a complete divorce between the functions of government and the holding of private property and wealth. The money-lovers will not want to rule, if to be a ruler means living in monastic austerity on a bare subsistence. Accordingly this mode of life is decreed for both the two higher classes. They are deprived of property, partly for their own sakes, lest the love of wealth should assert itself in them, but also for the sake of making the task of government a forbidding and disagreeable business in the eyes of the industrials.

These higher classes are also to be deprived of family life, for reasons which have been used in defence of the celibacy of the clergy. Where the family exists, the very strong instincts associated with marriage and fatherhood must absorb a large part of any normal man's interest and energy. Plato wanted to diffuse this energy over the whole class, and to abolish the distinction of mine and thine in this field, as in the field of property. On the other hand, if you select the most intellectual and spiritual men and women to form the head of your hierarchy, and then decree that they shall be childless, you inevitably impoverish the stock of the race. Plato avoids this sterilisation of the highest type by laying on his Guardians the duty of begetting children, who will not be their children, but the State's. A very carefully contrived system of arranged marriages is designed to meet the obvious objections.

These institutions are common to all the Guardians, as distinct from the industrials. The Guardians are then divided into two classes—the lovers of wisdom and the lovers of power. The ambitious type is not to be in control. They are to find their scope as the element of executive force in government and as the standing army. Here they will have sufficient play for their characteristic motive—the love of honour—and for their characteristic virtue, courage. All ultimate authority is reserved for the men of thought who have attained to wisdom and know what is the true end of human life. They will not desire to exercise authority; but they will undertake the direction of society as a duty which they alone can perform.

Towards the end of the *Republic* Plato seems to become more doubtful whether wisdom can ever be enthroned in human society. And if we could pass in review the long procession of kings and rulers who, since his time, have been responsible for the welfare of mankind, we might well think his doubts justified. Lord Russell has remarked that history presents no parallel so close to the Republic of Plato as the Bolshevik régime in Russia:

The Communist Party corresponds to the Guardians; the soldiers have about the same status in both; there is in Russia an attempt to deal with family life more or less as Plato suggested. I suppose it may be assumed that every teacher of Plato throughout the world abhors Bolshevism, and that every Bolshevik regards Plato as an antiquated *bourgeois*. Nevertheless, the parallel is extraordinarily exact between Plato's Republic and the régime which the better Bolsheviks are endeavouring to create.[1]

There is, of course, some truth in this. Both systems result from the conviction that society can be reformed only by subjecting the mass of mankind to the undisputed rule of a small minority, who are in possession of the truth and capable of a religious devotion to their task. Both systems are a consequence of the loss of belief

[1] *The Practice and Theory of Bolshevism* (1920), p. 30.

in democracy, which seems to be itself the consequence of a disastrous war. On the other hand, the philosophies which severally inspire the two systems are almost diametrically opposed; and I am inclined to think that the Bolsheviks are right if they regard Plato as an antiquated *bourgeois*, who would have repudiated dialectical materialism as founded on a false analysis of human nature.

Perhaps there is more truth in Wilamowitz's observation that, in the modern world, we find something comparable to Plato's State only in the structure of the Roman Church, culminating in the infallible authority of the triple crown. In Plato's latest work, the *Laws*, he tries to bring the institutions of the *Republic* closer to the given possibilities of actual life; and here there is a yet stronger resemblance to the Roman Church, which has found the secret of keeping a hold on human nature and has long outlived the Empire. In the institution of the Nocturnal Council, secretly watching over religion and morals, with powers of life and death, Plato has been said to have anticipated the Inquisition.

The likeness here is more than superficial. You will remember, in *The Brothers Karamazov*, Ivan's story of the Grand Inquisitor. An *auto-da-fé* has been held in Seville, in presence of the Cardinal and the court. Next day a stranger appears among the crowd in the market-place; and, though his coming is unobserved, he is instantly recognised. A healing virtue comes from the very touch of his garments. At the steps of the Cathedral he raises to life a child who is being brought to burial. In the confusion that follows, the Inquisitor passes by—an old man, tall and erect, with a withered face and sunken eyes, in which there is yet a gleam of light. He orders the arrest of the stranger, and at midnight visits him in the prison. He asks why he has come to hinder the work of the Church. The Church has relieved mankind of that intolerable burden of freedom, which the stranger had promised them. 'We have paid dearly for that promise', says the Inquisitor. 'For fifteen hundred years we have been wrestling with that freedom, and now it is ended. The people have brought their freedom to us, and laid it humbly at our feet.' The Church has given them, instead of freedom, authority; instead of knowledge, mystery. And men rejoiced that they were again led like sheep. The terrible gift that had brought so much suffering was at last lifted from their hearts.

The stranger makes no answer. At the end he suddenly goes up to the old man and kisses him. The Inquisitor opens the prison door upon the dark streets, telling him to go, and never to come again. Afterwards, the memory of that kiss glows in the old man's heart, but he holds to his conviction.

If the ideal State of the *Laws* had ever become a living reality, we might imagine a parallel scene: Socrates arraigned for a second trial before the Nocturnal Council, and confronted with Plato in the president's chair. Socrates had held out the same gift of unlimited freedom and self-rule; and Plato had foreseen that mankind would not be able to bear it. So he devised this commonwealth, that the few who are wise might keep the conscience of the many who will never be wise.

But I cannot imagine the end of my story. All that I am sure of is that Plato's prisoner, unlike the Inquisitor's, would not have kept an unbroken silence.

THE DOCTRINE OF EROS IN
PLATO'S *SYMPOSIUM*

THE *Symposium* is held to be near in date to the *Phaedo*, in which the deliverance of Socrates by a self-chosen death from the Athenian prison becomes the symbol of the deliverance of man's soul from the prison-house of the body by its own passion for wisdom. Whichever of the two dialogues was finished first—and I suspect it was the *Phaedo*—Plato felt the need to hang beside the picture it gave of Socrates another picture as different as possible.

Every genuine drama has a physical atmosphere. The storm is as necessary to *King Lear* as the stillness after storm is to *The Tempest*. The atmosphere of the *Phaedo* is the twilight that precedes the night: 'the sun is still upon the mountains; he has not yet gone down'. It ends at sunset, with Socrates' mythical discourse about an Earthly Paradise for purified souls. The atmosphere of the *Symposium* is steeped in the brilliant light of Agathon's banquet, celebrating the victory of his play in the theatre. Socrates on his arrival, replying to the poet's welcome, speaks of his own wisdom as 'a sorry thing, questionable, like a dream; but you are young, and your wisdom is bright and full of promise—that wisdom which, two days ago, shone out before the eyes of more than thirty thousand Greeks'. And the *Symposium* ends at daybreak, with Socrates arguing with the two drowsy poets till they fall asleep and he goes off to take a bath and to argue all the rest of the day at the Lyceum.

The *Phaedo* had brought out the ascetic strain in Socrates, the man of thought to whom the body with its senses and appetites is at best a nuisance. There was that strain in him. The Cynics were destined to fasten upon it and follow the track that leads from the denial of the flesh to a point where the sage will be found taking refuge in a dog-kennel—the tub of Diogenes ὁ κύων—and advertising his singular virtue by outraging not only the graces but the decencies of life. Plato's word for such men is ἄμουσος—uncultivated, ungracious, unmusical. Socrates was not such, but rather the chief and indispensable guest at the elegant young poet's table. If he was a man of superhuman self-restraint, that was not because there was nothing in his nature to restrain. He could drink more wine than anyone else, but no one had ever seen him drunk. He had not, as some later critics said, ignored or 'abolished' the passionate side of human nature; he had done something else with it. The man of thought was also the man of passion, constantly calling himself a 'lover', not in the vulgar sense—the speech of Alcibiades was to make that perfectly clear—but still a lover. The *Symposium* is to explain the significance of Eros to the lover of wisdom.

In the *Republic* Plato divides the soul into three parts: the reflective or rational, the spirited or passionate, and the concupiscent; and he defines the several virtues of wisdom, courage, temperance, and justice as they appear in the complex nature of man in his present state of imperfection. An essential point of this triple division is that each so-called 'part' of the soul is characterised by a peculiar form of desire. Moreover, these three forms of desire are themselves characterised by their peculiar objects. Thus, where Plato proves that the tyrannical man is of all men most miserable, he observes that each part of the soul has its own pleasure and its own characteristic desire and any one of the three may take control. The reflective part desires understanding and wisdom; the passionate aims at success, honour, and power; the concupiscent is so called because of the special intensity of the desires of nutrition and sex; it is acquisitive, loving money as a means to sensual gratification. There are, accordingly, three main types of human character determined by the dominance of one or another desire, three lives seeking respectively the pleasures of the contemplation of truth, of contentious ambition, and of material gain. The inferior pleasures are declared to be in some sense false and illusory. On the other hand, the two lower parts are not to be merely crushed and repressed. They will be positively better off, in respect of their own satisfaction, under the rule of reason than when left to themselves. And conversely, if either of the lower parts usurps control, not only does it force the others to pursue false pleasures, but it does not even find the truest satisfaction of which it is itself capable. In this respect the lowest is the worst. A life dominated by unchecked sensual indulgence is the least pleasant of all.

Hence it appears that we are not to think of the soul as divided into reason, a thinking part, on the one side, and irrational appetite on the other; or of the internal conflict as between passionless reason, always in the right, and passion and desire, usually in the wrong. That analysis would point to an ascetic morality of the repression and mortification of the flesh, the extinction of passion and desire, leaving only dispassionate contemplation. Much of the *Phaedo* suggests a morality of that type; but there what is called 'the soul' is only the highest of the three parts, which alone is immortal; the other parts are called 'the body' or the flesh. The *Phaedo* is concerned with death and its significance for the perfect man. For him philosophy is a rehearsal of death, and death is deliverance from the flesh. But the *Republic* is concerned with this life and the best that can be made of our composite nature, in which all three forms of desire claim their legitimate satisfaction. Hence the conception of virtue is centred in the notion of a harmony of desires—a condition in which each part pursues its appropriate pleasure and finds its truest satisfaction, without thwarting or perverting the others. There is for each type of man one best possible balance or harmony of various desires. The condition may not be perfect; but it is more stable and happier than any other.

Beyond this lies an ideal solution, which would produce the perfect individual. In the later books of the *Republic* that solution is stated on the intellectual side. There is a higher education which might end in perfect knowledge and fashion the only type of man who ought to take control of human society—the philosopher-king. But the process is not purely intellectual; it involves the education of desire. This aspect is developed in the *Symposium*, in the theory of Eros, the name for the impulse of desire in all its forms. We are now to learn that the three impulses which shape three types of life are not ultimately distinct and irreducible factors, residing in three separate parts of a composite soul, or some in the soul, some in the body. They are manifestations of a single force or fund of energy, called Eros, directed through divergent channels towards various ends. This conception makes possible a sublimation of desire; the energy can be redirected from one channel to another. The flow can be diverted upwards or downwards. The downward process is analysed in the eighth and ninth books of the *Republic*. It leads to the hell of sensuality in the tyrannical man. The upward process is indicated in the *Symposium*.

I must pass over the earlier speeches, which contribute suggestions about the nature of Eros that are either taken up or criticised in the discourse of Socrates. Last of the six speakers, Socrates follows after Agathon, the poet, who has given a sentimental and euphuistic panegyric of Eros as personified by the artist's imagination. Agathon professes to describe 'the nature of Eros himself', the most blessed of the gods, fairest and youngest, delicate and soft in form. He has every virtue: he is just, as neither doing nor suffering injustice; temperate, as the master of all pleasures, for no pleasure is stronger than Love; brave, for Ares himself cannot resist him; and wise, transforming anyone whom he touches into a poet.

Socrates then opens with a conversational criticism of Agathon. By a masterstroke of delicate courtesy he avoids making his host look foolish. He pretends that he himself had spoken of Eros in similar terms to Diotima, a wise priestess of Mantinea, and he represents the criticism as administered by Diotima to himself. This is a sufficient reason for the invention of Diotima. Socrates, moreover, can put forward the whole doctrine not as his own, but as hers, and so escape professing to know more about Eros than his fellow-guests.

Agathon's description of Eros as graced with every beauty and virtue is not a description of Eros at all, but of the object of Eros. Beauty and goodness are attributes, not of desire, but of the thing desired. This criticism points to a curious phenomenon of personification. The representations of Aphrodite and Eros in highly developed art, as an ideally beautiful woman and youth, are representations of the desirable, not of Desire—of the lovable, not of Love. Henceforward it will be assumed that the object of Eros, in all its forms from lowest to highest, is something that can be called either the beautiful or the good, indifferently. Beauty and goodness may be manifested in a variety of forms, ranging through the whole scale of being. It is this variety of forms that distinguishes the several kinds of desire; but the passion itself is fundamentally the same.

Diotima had put the same argument to Socrates: that desire must lack that which it desires; but she had added that, if Eros lacks beauty and goodness, it does not follow that he is ugly and bad. He may be neither good nor bad. In mythical terms, Eros is neither god nor mortal, but a *daimon* intermediate between the two—one of those spirits through whom intercourse between the divine and mortal worlds is maintained. For the object of Eros is to be found in both worlds, the seen and the unseen; here there is visible beauty, a likeness of the invisible beauty yonder; and Eros lends to Psyche the wings that will carry her across the boundary. But the point here is that desire, in itself, is neutral, neither good nor bad; it takes its value from its object.

This object is first described in general terms: Eros is the desire for the possession of beauty and goodness, that is to say, of happiness. This desire is universal: 'All have a passion for the same things always.' The name Eros has been wrongly restricted in common speech to what is really only one form of this universal desire. Just as the word 'making' (ποίησις) really means creation of any kind, but has been misappropriated to one species—metrical composition, poetry—so the name of Eros is misappropriated to one species of passion, but really means 'any and every desire for good things and for happiness'. Diotima next alludes to the three types of life. Those who turn to seek it in many other directions, some in getting wealth, some in athletic pursuits, others in the pursuit of wisdom, are not called 'lovers' nor said to be 'in love'; the name has been usurped by those whose energy passes into one special form.

From this conception of a common fund of moving force Plato elsewhere draws an inference, based on experience. The amount of energy directed into one channel is withdrawn from the others, as if only a limited quantity were available. In the *Republic* (588 B) the soul is imaged as a composite creature, part man, part lion, part many-headed monster. One who praises injustice is saying that it is profitable to feed and strengthen the multifarious monster and to starve and enfeeble the man, so as to leave him at the mercy of the other two. Again (485), where the language of Eros is used to define the philosophic nature by its essential passion for truth, the metaphor of channels is used. 'When a person's desires are set strongly in one direction, we know that they flow with corresponding feebleness in every other, like a stream whose waters have been diverted into a different channel. Accordingly when the flow of desires has set towards knowledge in all its forms, a man's desire will be turned to the pleasures which the soul has by itself and will abandon the pleasures of the body, if his love of wisdom be not feigned.' Socrates then goes on to explain how the whole character is shaped by this master passion.

We can now see more clearly how virtue of the ordinary kind, the harmony of desires in the complex nature, is effected by the readjustment of natural impulses. During this life the energy must flow along all the channels in due measure. Some part must go to preserve mortal life. The pleasure attached to bodily functions attracts the necessary force, and is innocent, if controlled and not mistaken for the end of life. Another part must go into the interests and duties of civic life. So the love of power is satisfied and rewarded with the honours bestowed by society. And the love of truth and goodness will be satisfied in the exercise of prudence or practical wisdom. The harmony of the three elements will be achieved by a right distribution of the available energy.

But this is not the end of the matter, or of Diotima's discourse. She now defines the common object of all desire as the possession of the good, with the significant addition 'for ever'. How can this be attained by the mortal creature? By means of the characteristic operation of love, generation. In all human beings there is the urge to bring to birth children, whether of the body or of the mind. The end is not the individual's immediate enjoyment of beauty, but the perpetuation of life by the creative act, to which Beauty ministers, like a birth-goddess, giving release from travail.

Procreation is the divine attribute in the mortal animal. Eros is, in the last resort, the desire for immortality.

Even in its lower forms Eros betrays this divine quality, whereby it reaches out to something beyond its immediate and apparent object—beyond any personal happiness that can be achieved and enjoyed during the individual's life. At its lowest level, in the animal form of sex-passion, its aim is the immortality of the species. 'Have you not perceived', says Diotima, 'that all animals are strangely affected when the desire comes upon them to produce offspring? They are all distraught with passion, first for union with one another and then for rearing the young creature: and for its sake the weakest will fight with the strongest and lay down their lives, or they will starve themselves to feed their young; there is nothing they will not do.' The reason is that the mortal nature seeks, within the limit of its power, to exist for ever and to be immortal. This it can achieve, not in its own person, but by leaving behind a new thing in place of the old. All mortal life is a perpetual renewal and change, not unchanging like the divine. This is the only immortality possible for the mortal race.

Discussing marriage regulations in his last work, the *Laws*, Plato writes: 'It is a man's duty to marry, remembering that there is a sense in which the human race by nature partakes of immortality—a thing for which the desire is implanted in man in all its forms; for the desire to be famous and not to lie nameless in the grave is a desire for immortality. The race of man is twin-born with all time and follows its course in a companionship that will endure to the end; and it is immortal in this way—by leaving children's children, so that the race remains always one and the same and partakes of immortality by means of generation' (721 B).

This passage mentions the desire for the immortality of fame. Diotima passes on to this: 'If you consider human ambition, you will marvel at its irrationality, unless you reflect on what I have said, and observe how strangely men are moved by the passion for winning a name, and laying up undying glory for all time.' This form of Eros is characteristic of the passionate or spirited part of the soul. Usually we think of the ambitions of this part as directed to the worldly success and advancement of the individual.

But here also desire reaches out to an immortality which the individual can never enjoy, and for this he will sacrifice all that he can enjoy and life itself.

There is, moreover, a third way in which the individual can perpetuate something of himself, namely by begetting children, not of his body, but of his mind. Of this kind are poets and creative artists, whose works survive and carry their thoughts to posterity. Still more the educator begets children of a fairer and more lasting kind, by planting his thoughts in living minds, where they will live again, to beget yet other generations of spiritual children. And with the educator is ranked the lawgiver—Lycurgus or Solon—who leaves laws and institutions as permanent means of training his fellow-citizens in virtue.

At this point Diotima pauses and says: 'Into these lesser mysteries of Eros, you, Socrates, may perhaps be initiated; but I know not whether you are capable of the perfect revelation—the goal to which they lead. I will not fail, on my part, to express it as well as I can; you must try to follow, to the best of your power.' I incline to agree with those scholars who have seen in this sentence Plato's intention to mark the limit reached by the philosophy of his master. Socrates had been the prince of those educators who can beget spiritual children in others' minds and help them to bring their own thoughts to birth. Had he gone further? Immortality in all the three forms so far described is immortality of the mortal creature, who may perpetuate his race, his fame, his thoughts, in another. The individual himself does not survive; he dies, and leaves something behind. This is immortality in time, not in an eternal world. All that is contained in the lesser mysteries is true, even if there be no other world, no enduring existence for any element in the individual soul. The disclosure of the other world—the eternal realm of the Ideas—is reserved for the greater mysteries that follow. If I am right in believing that Socrates' philosophy was a philosophy of life in this world, while Plato's was centred in another world, here is the point where they part company.

The line which here divides the lesser from the greater mysteries corresponds to the division between the two stages of education described in the *Republic*: the lower education in gymnastic and music of the earlier books and the higher education of the philosopher in Book VII. In the *Republic* the transition is obscured by a long intervening discussion of other matters; the *Symposium* supplies the link. The end of that lower musical education was to produce in the soul reasonableness, harmony, rhythm, simplicity of character. These are likenesses, existing in individual souls, of the eternal Ideas of Temperance, Courage, and the other virtues. Such an image is, for him who can discern it, the noblest object of contemplation, and also the loveliest: it inspires Eros in the musical man, the love of the individual person in whom these images of goodness dwell. So music ends, where it should end, in the passion for beauty, not a passion for sensual pleasure. From this point the greater mysteries of the *Symposium* start. They describe the conversion of Eros from the love of a single beautiful and noble person to the love of the Beautiful itself. They correspond to the higher intellectual education of the *Republic*, where the eye of the soul is converted from the idols of the Cave to the upper world of sunlight and finally to the vision of the Good. In this last transformation Eros becomes a passion for immortality, not in time, but in the region of the eternal.

There are four stages in this progress. The first step is the detachment of Eros from the individual person and from physical beauty. The individual object is lost sight of in the realisation that all physical beauty is one and the same, in whatsoever individual it may appear.

The passions [writes Mr Santayana], in so far as they are impulses to action, entangle us materially in the flux of substance, being intent on seizing, transforming, or destroying something that exists; but at the same time, in so far as they quicken the mind, they are favourable to the discernment of essence; and it is only a passionate soul that can be truly contemplative. The reward of the lover, which also chastens him, is to discover that, in thinking he loved anything of this world, he was profoundly mistaken. Everybody strives for possession; that is the animal instinct on which everything hangs; but possession leaves the true lover unsatisfied: his joy is in the character of the thing loved, in the essence it reveals, whether it be here or there, now or then, his or another's. This essence, which for action was only a signal letting loose a generic animal impulse, to contemplation is the whole object of love, and the sole gain in loving.[1]

Next, we must learn to value moral beauty in the mind above beauty of the body, and to contemplate the unity and kinship of all that is honourable and noble—a constant meaning of τὸ καλόν—in law and conduct.

The third stage reveals intellectual beauty in the mathematical sciences. Eros now becomes the philosophic impulse to grasp abstract truth and to discover that kind of beauty which the geometer finds in a theorem and the astronomer in the harmonious order of the heavenly bodies. By now we have lost sight of individual objects and the temporal images of beauty, and we have entered the intelligible world.

The final object—beyond physical, moral, and intellectual beauty—is the Beautiful itself. This is revealed to intuition 'suddenly'. The language here recalls the culminating revelation of the Eleusinian mysteries—the disclosure of sacred symbols or figures of the divinities in a sudden blaze of light. This object is eternal, exempt from change and relativity, no longer manifested in anything else, in any living thing, or in earth or heaven, but always 'by itself', entirely unaffected by the becoming or perishing of anything that may partake of its character. The act of acquaintance with it is the vision of a spectacle, whereby the soul has contact with the ultimate object of Eros and enters into possession of it. So man becomes immortal in the divine sense. As in the *Republic*, the union of the soul with Beauty is called a marriage—the sacred marriage of the Eleusinia—of which the offspring are, not phantoms like those images of goodness that first inspired love of the beautiful person, but true virtue, the virtue which is wisdom. For Plato believed that the goal of philosophy was that man should become a god, knowing good from evil with such clearness and certainty as could not fail to determine the will infallibly.

The final act of knowledge is described as an immediate intuition in which there is no longer any process of thought. The eye of the soul directly contemplates reality. We may, and perhaps

[1] G. Santayana, *The Realm of Essence* (Constable, 1928), p. 116.

must, conjecture that the description is based on some experience which Plato had at privileged moments. There is no warrant in tradition for supposing that he ever passed into a condition of trance or ecstasy. The Neoplatonists would have seized eagerly on any such tradition, had it existed in the school. He uses the language of the Eleusinian mysteries because it is appropriate to a sudden vision led up to by a long process of instruction and initiation. But the revelation at Eleusis, of course, no more involved ecstasy than does the elevation of the host. Perhaps Plato's experience should be called metaphysical, rather than religious—a recognition of ultimate truth. On the other hand, it is not purely intellectual, but a conversion of every element in the soul by the last trans-figuration of Eros: and at that point the distinction between the metaphysical and the religious may become meaningless.

To return to the theory of Eros: the energy which carries the soul in this highest flight is the same that is manifested at lower levels in the instinct that perpetuates the race and in every form of worldly ambition. It is the energy of life itself, the moving force of the soul; and the soul was defined by Plato precisely as the one thing that has the power of self-motion. The Platonic doctrine of Eros has been compared, and even identified, with modern theories of sublimation. But the ultimate standpoints of Plato and of Freud seem to be diametrically opposed. Modern science is dominated by the concept of evolution, the upward development from the rude and primitive instincts of our alleged animal ancestry to the higher manifestations of rational life. The conception was not foreign to Greek thought. The earliest philo-sophical school had taught that man had developed from a fish-like creature, spawned in the slime warmed by the heat of the sun. But Plato had deliberately rejected this system of thought. Man is for him the plant whose roots are not in earth but in the heavens. In the myth of transmigration the lower animals are deformed and degraded types, in which the soul which has not been true to its celestial affinity may be imprisoned to work out the penalty of its fall. The self-moving energy of the human soul resides properly in the highest part, the immortal nature. It does not rise from beneath, but rather sinks from above when the spirit is ensnared in the flesh. So, when the energy is withdrawn from the lower channels, it is gathered up into its original source. This is indeed a conversion or transfiguration; but not a sublimation of desire that has hitherto existed only in the lower forms. A force that was in origin spiritual, after an incidental and temporary declension, becomes purely spiritual again. The opposition to Freud is not merely due to misunderstanding and prejudice. It is due to the fact that the religious consciousness of Christianity has been, almost from the first, under the influence of Platonism.

I adopted the view that Diotima's words to Socrates on the threshold of the greater mysteries, where she doubts if he can follow her further, indicate that Plato is going beyond the historic Socrates. It has been objected that this interpretation makes Plato 'guilty of the arrogance of professing that he has reached philosophical heights to which the historical Socrates could not ascend'. But the best commentary on the *Symposium* is to be found in the *Divine Comedy*. Dante, as a man, was far more arrogant than Plato; but it was not arrogance that made him represent Virgil as taking leave of him at the threshold of the Earthly Paradise, before his flight from Earth to Heaven. Dante has passed the seven circles of Purgatory and is now purified of sin. Virgil, who has guided him so far, stands for human wisdom or philosophy, which can lead to the Earthly Paradise, but not to the Heavenly. The analogy is not complete. Dante's guide to the higher region is the Christian revelation, the divine wisdom symbolised by Beatrice—not a further development of human philosophy, but a God-given addition. But if there is some analogy, Plato might mean that his own philosophy, centred in another world, lay beyond the explicit doctrine of his master, though it might be implicit in his life and practice. That is not to deny that Socrates was the ideal philosopher, who lived (though he never taught) what Plato intends to teach. Nor is it to say that Plato claimed to be a greater philosopher than Socrates, any more than Dante claimed to be a better poet than Virgil.

However that may be, Virgil's farewell words exactly express the doctrine of Eros:[1]

[1] *Purgatorio*, Canto xxvii, lines 115 ff.

> This day the sweet fruit which mortals seek on so many branches will set thy hunger at rest.

The sweet fruit is happiness which men pursue under so many guises. At these words,

> Desire upon desire of being above so came to me that at every step thereafter I felt my wings grow for the flight.

These are the wings which Psyche receives from Eros—the wings of her own desire.

> When the whole stair was passed and now beneath us, and we were on the topmost step, Virgil fixed his eyes upon me, and said: 'My son, thou hast seen the temporal fire and the eternal, and thou art come to a place where, of myself, I see no further. I have led thee hither with intelligence and art; henceforward take thine own pleasure for guide; thou hast come forth of the steep and narrow ways.

> See there the Sun, which shines upon thy forehead; see the tender grass, the flowers, the young trees which here the Earth of herself alone brings forth.

> While those fair eyes with joy are shining, whose weeping made me come to thee, here mayst thou sit and walk among them.

> Await no more word or sign from me. Free, right and sound is thine own will; and not to act according to its prompting would be a fault.

> Therefore I give thee, over thyself, the mitre and the crown.

The mitre and the crown are the signs of sovereignty, spiritual and temporal. Dante, now purified, is subject to no external power; because his own will has become right, sound and free, and cannot lead him astray. Hence he is made priest and king over himself.

So the *Republic* calls the perfect philosopher 'the most royal of kings, who is king over himself'; but not until he has climbed the steep and narrow way out of the Cave, to see the Good, like a sun shining upon his forehead, and has learnt what it is that makes man's life worth living.

GREEK NATURAL PHILOSOPHY
AND MODERN SCIENCE

W HEN I was invited to contribute to this course[1] a
single lecture on Greek Philosophy and Science, my
first impulse was to reply: Greek philosophy began
when Thales of Miletus successfully predicted an eclipse of the sun
in 585 B.C. and ended in A.D. 529 when the Christian Emperor
Justinian closed the schools of Athens. What can I say, in fifty
minutes, about a development of thought which covered eleven
centuries—a longer span than separates ourselves from the reign
of King Alfred?

Plainly, I must limit myself to a few general considerations.
Of these the most relevant will be the differences distinguishing
the Greek study of Nature from the natural science of our modern
period. These differences are obvious on the surface, but the underlying reasons for them may easily be overlooked. The man of
science to-day works at his own field within the horizon of a
certain outlook, and using a certain apparatus of concepts which
are the common property of his contemporaries. If he is not a
philosopher or a psychologist, he may tacitly assume that this outlook and this apparatus are the only possible ones and have always
been common property, imposed upon any student of Nature by
Nature herself. He may then be puzzled, if he should dip into the
pages of Aristotle or Lucretius. He may there light upon some
startling anticipations of recent discoveries, but he will find them
embedded in a mass of what looks to him like nonsense. He may
conclude that the ancients were like clever children, with some
bright ideas, but with untrained minds, who had advanced only
a little way along the one right approach to truth.

This illusion is rampant in histories of philosophy and science.
It is fostered by writers on the classics who catch at every chance

[1] A series of lectures on the background to modern science, arranged by
the Cambridge University History of Science Committee in 1936.

of showing that the past they love is not out of date. But one purpose of this course of lectures should be to point out that the ancients were not moderns in the stage of infancy or adolescence. The Graeco-Roman culture was a self-contained growth, with its own infancy, adolescence, maturity, and decay. After the Dark Age and the Middle Ages, the modern science of Nature starts at the Renaissance with a fresh motive impulse. The questions it asks are different questions. Its method is a new method, dictated by the need to meet those new questions with an appropriate answer.

You know better than I do what you are trying to find out here in your laboratories, and how and why you go about your task. I am told that you proceed by a method of tentative hypotheses, suggested by careful observation of facts, and controlled by no less careful experiment. Your objective has been described (at least till very recently) as the discovery of laws of cause and effect, invariable sequences of phenomena. And your motive—what is your motive? Shall we say: a pure and dispassionate love of truth for its own sake? I will accept that answer gladly; long may it remain as true as it is now in Cambridge. But there are some people who think that truth is the same thing as usefulness, and that the study of Nature really aims at the control of natural forces as a means to a further end. Some, again, would define that end as the increase of wealth and material comfort, and increase of power, which may itself be used to destroy, not only the comfort, but the lives, of our competitors in the scramble for wealth. Hence the subsidies lavished on natural science by War Departments and captains of industry. Hence the unabashed emergence of Nordic physics in central Europe and of proletarian physics farther east. Your very protons and electrons are suspected of capitalist or Marxian sympathies. Your neutrons are not to be politically neutral.

Now if that is a roughly true picture of natural science in the last four centuries, it differs in every respect—in method, in objective, and in underlying impulse—from the physical speculation of antiquity. My purpose is to bring out these differences and to raise, if I cannot wholly answer, the question why they exist.

First, let me indicate the limits of my subject. Other speakers are to deal with Greek mathematics and biology. 'Science and Philosophy' in the title of this lecture must be taken to mean what the Greeks called Physics or 'the inquiry into the nature of things'. In this field all the most important and original work was done in the three centuries from 600 to 300 B.C. After Aristotle's death in 322 physics fell into the background; philosophers became preoccupied with the quest of a moral or religious faith that would make human life bearable. In those first three centuries no line was drawn distinguishing philosophy from the study of Nature. Before Aristotle there were no separate branches of natural science. The word for science (knowledge, ἐπιστήμη) was applied rather to mathematics, because mathematics deals with exactly defined unchanging objects and demonstrable truths, and so could claim to yield knowledge in the fullest sense. Physics was known as 'the inquiry into the nature of things'. We should speak of it rather by its older name, natural philosophy. Accordingly, we are now concerned only with the natural philosophy of the period ending with the school of Aristotle.

Let us begin with method and procedure. In this period, down to and including Aristotle's master, Plato, philosophy perpetuated the traditional form of exposition—the cosmogonical myth, a narrative describing the birth or formation of an ordered universe. Such myths are found all over the world, in societies where science has never begun to exist. They exhibit two main patterns, singly or in combination: the evolutionary and the creational. In the one the world is born and grows like a living creature; in the other it is designed and fashioned like a work of art. The formula is familiar: 'In the beginning the earth was without form and void; and darkness was upon the face of the deep.' Or, in more refined language: 'In the beginning was an indefinite incoherent homogeneity.' The initial assumption is that the complex, differentiated world we see has somehow arisen out of a state of things which was both simple and disorderly.

The earliest Greek school at Miletus in the sixth century followed the evolutionary scheme. The original condition of things was water or mist. Cosmogony then proceeds to tell how this primitive moisture was condensed to form the solid core of earth, and rarefied into the encompassing air and the heavenly fires. Then, within this elemental order, life was born in the slime warmed by the sun's heat. This evolutionary tradition culminated in the Atomism of Democritus, towards the end of the fifth century. His system, with slight modifications, was adopted, after Aristotle's death, by Epicurus, and reproduced by Lucretius for the Roman public in the first century B.C. For Democritus the original state of things was a chaos of minute solid bodies, moving incalculably in all directions in a void, colliding, and forming vortices in which ordered worlds arise, by necessity and chance without design. There are innumerable worlds, some being formed, others falling to pieces, scattered through unlimited empty space.

The alternative pattern, preferred by Plato for moral and religious reasons, is the creational. The world is like a thing not born but made, containing evidences of intelligent and intelligible design. Necessity and chance play only a subordinate part, subdued (though not completely subdued) to the purposes of a divine Reason. For convenience Plato retained the old narrative form of exposition; but neither he nor Aristotle believed that the cosmos had any beginning in time or will ever come to an end. So Plato's myth of creation in the *Timaeus* is really a disguised analysis of the complex world into simpler factors, not a literal history of its development from a disorderly condition that once actually existed.

For Plato and Aristotle there is only one world, a spherical universe bounded by the fixed stars. Plato held that it was animated by a World-Soul, whose intelligence is responsible for those elements of rational order which we can discern in the structure. Blind necessity and chance are also at work, producing results which no good intelligence could desire; but they are in some degree subordinated to co-operate with benevolent Reason. For this Reason Aristotle substitutes a vaguely personified Nature, who always aims at some end.

Now, whichever of the two patterns be adopted—the evolutionary or the creational—cosmogony deals dogmatically with matters wholly beyond the reach of direct observation. You must, indeed, look at the world to see that there is a solid earth at the centre, surrounded by layers of water, air, and fire; but no one had observed the primitive disorderly condition, or how order arose from it, and life came to be born. Nor did it occur to the ancients that their imaginative reconstruction of the past could be checked by any experimental test. For example, Anaximenes, the third philosopher of the Milesian School, held that as the primitive air or mist passed from the gaseous state to the liquid, as water, and from the liquid to the solid, as earth and stones, it became colder and also denser, more closely packed. On this showing ice ought to take up less room than water. But Anaximenes never set out a jar of water on a frosty night so as to find out how much the water would shrink when turned to ice. The result would have surprised him. It is still stranger to our minds that no critic should have thought of confirming or confuting him by this means.

This neglect of experiment is connected with the traditional form of exposition. Physical theories were stated, not as hypotheses, but as a narrative of what happened in the remotest past: 'In the beginning' there was water, or mist, or qualities like hot and cold, or atoms of definite sizes and shapes. Who could decide which of these accounts was to be preferred? A physicist could do little more than accuse others of inconsistency; he could not prove his own doctrine to be true. 'We are all inclined', says Aristotle, 'to direct our inquiry not by the matter itself, but by the views of our opponents; and, even when interrogating oneself, one pushes the inquiry only to the point at which one can no longer find any objections' (*De Caelo* 294 B 7). On the other hand, these early philosophers did good service by thinking out a number of alternative possibilities, some of which might bear fruit later. Atomism, which has recently borne astonishing fruit, might not have been thought of, if Democritus had not allowed his reason to outrun his senses, and assert a reality which the senses can never perceive, and no means of observation then existing could verify.

So much for differences of method. My second point is the difference in objective: what it was that the ancients were bent upon discovering.

Both types of cosmogony can be regarded as answering the question: what things really and ultimately *are*? Suppose you say that the objects we see around us are compounds of earth, water, air, and fire, and that earth, water and fire themselves were originally formed from air, by condensation or rarefaction. You will then hold that everything now really and ultimately consists of air, in different states of density. Or you may say that everything really consists of atoms. On these lines the evolutionary type of cosmogony will declare that the real nature of things is to be found in their matter. Your philosophy will then be materialistic; and you may go on to say (as Democritus did) that the soul consists of specially mobile spherical atoms, and that all our thoughts and feelings are to be explained in terms of the motions and collisions of minute impenetrable bodies. To some this may sound fantastic; but there are still people who would like to believe something of the sort, and there are signs that the Epicurean philosophy is again becoming popular.

To this question of the real nature of things, the creational type returned a different answer. It found this real nature, not in the matter, but in the form. That was because it looked on the world as a product of craftsmanship; and the essence of such products lies in their form.

A potter is moulding clay. You ask, what is this thing he is making? A teapot. What is a teapot? A vessel with a spout to pour the tea through, a lid to keep it hot, and a handle to hold the thing by without burning your fingers. You now understand the nature of the object in the light of the purpose dictating its essential features. The material is not essential: you can make a teapot of clay or of silver or of any rigid stuff that holds liquid. The essence or real being or substance of the thing is its form. Now suppose that the world is like a teapot in being a work of design. Matter will then exist for the sake of the form that is to be realized. The essence of living creatures will be the perfect form into which they grow. It is manifest in the full-grown tree, not in the seed. The real nature must be sought in the end, not in the beginning, and the end irresistibly suggests the aim of conscious or unconscious purpose. This type of cosmology reached its perfection in Plato and Aristotle, in deliberate opposition to materialism.

But whether the answer be matter or form, both types tell us what things really *are*; they do not confine themselves to the question, how things *behave*. Here is the second point of difference between ancient and modern natural philosophy. At all times the quest is for something permanent, and therefore knowable, in the ceaseless flow of appearances. For the ancients this permanent something is substance, whether substance be understood as tangible material substance or as the intangible essence of the specific form.

Aristotle takes both into account: he speaks of the material and formal 'causes' of things. Neither is a 'cause' in our sense of the word. They are the two constituents, which answer the question: what *is* this thing? The moderns, on the other hand, are concerned, not so much with what things are, as with how they behave. By a cause we mean some phenomenon or event which regularly precedes some other phenomenon or event, called its 'effect'. We are looking for those invariable connections or sequences which are known as 'laws of nature'. Such laws do not describe the internal nature of things, but rather the constant relations between them.

Why was there this difference of objective—the ancients defining the substance of things, the moderns formulating sequences of events? One reason was that, for the ancients, the pre-eminent science, setting the pattern of all organised knowledge, was geometry. Geometry alone had developed a method and technique of establishing necessary truths—proving conclusions that must be accepted by anyone who accepted the premisses. And the method of geometrical reasoning was leading to a continual and triumphant progress in discovery. No wonder that the search for something certain and knowable in the physical world should follow this brilliant example and unconsciously imitate its methods.

Now geometry is not at all concerned to describe the sequence of events in time. It has no use for observation or experiment. It starts from a definition, stating, for instance, what the triangle essentially is. It then goes on to deduce from that definition and a few other explicit premisses, a whole string of necessary properties of the triangle: its angles are equal to two right angles, and so on. If you can exhaust these necessary properties, you will know all that can be known about the triangle. When, with that ideal of knowledge in mind, you turn to the physical world, you will be disposed to inquire after the essential nature of visible and tangible things, and to enumerate their necessary properties, in the hope of knowing all that can be known about them. You may then develop a technique of definition by generic and specific differences. What is a man? Plainly he falls under the genus Animal, as the triangle falls under the genus Plane Figure. What is the essential or specific difference, distinguishing man from other animals, as the triangle is distinguished from other figures by having three sides? Man is a biped; but so is a goose. We must add another difference, 'featherless', or perhaps 'rational', to distinguish man from birds. So a genus is divided into species by a method of classification, which was first elaborated by Plato and which still persists in zoology and botany. The procedure answers the ancient question: What is the essential nature of this thing?

Aristotle tries to reduce to this pattern even such questions as the cause of an eclipse of the moon. He treats 'eclipse', not as an event, following upon some earlier event called its cause, but as an attribute of the moon. The moon is the subject, and when you state the fact that it is eclipsed, you are saying that it has the attribute 'eclipse'. If you then ask for the reason—Why has the moon this attribute?—the answer will be the same as if you ask for a definition of 'eclipse'. 'It is clear', he writes, 'that the nature of the thing and the reason of the fact are identical. The question "What is an eclipse?" and its answer: "Privation of the moon's light by the interposition of the earth", are the same as the question: "Why is there an eclipse?" and the answer: "Because of the failure of light when the earth is interposed".' Thus the inquiry for the cause of an event is reduced to inquiry for the definition of an attribute. We ask: What is the essential nature of an eclipse? just as we asked: What is the essential nature of a triangle or a man?

Aristotle is not setting out a sequence of two events, one of which precedes the other and brings it about. What moderns call the 'cause'—the interposition of the earth—is to Aristotle part of the definition of an affection suffered occasionally by the moon.

This manner of approach has a further consequence. When we pass from the abstract and timeless objects of geometry to the changing things in this visible world, we find that individual men, unlike the triangle, have also many properties that are not essential. A man may be tall or short, white or black, wise or foolish. Besides the essential core of properties, without any one of which he would not be a man at all, there is, in any particular man, a fringe of attributes which he may or may not have, may acquire or lose without ceasing to be human. These attributes are called 'accidental' or 'contingent', as opposed to 'essential' and 'necessary'. If your object is to define the universal essence common to all men, you will rule out these accidental properties of individuals as beyond the scope of knowledge. And the words 'accidental', 'contingent' suggest chance—what is not determined one way or the other, but may or may not be so. The notion of chance is very obscure, and I cannot pursue it; but I believe that ancient views of the world allowed more scope for chance than is commonly recognised.

If so, that is because the ancients were not thinking of Nature, as we think, in terms of invariable laws of cause and effect. When you arrive at that notion, chance must disappear. Every event must have another event before it as cause, and before that yet another, and so on for ever. Order and Necessity will now cover the whole field, usurping the old domain of the accidental, contingent, disorderly, unknowable. So the belief in universal law led modern science to complete determinism. Miracles were not to happen. The gods were either eliminated or pushed back to an imaginary beginning, with the honorary title of First Cause—honorary, because no one really believed that there could be such a thing as a first cause. And man himself was asked to surrender the inveterate belief in his own freedom, lest he should break in upon the chain of necessary events and start a fresh and unpredictable series. In order that Nature may work like a perfect machine, man must keep in his place as a part of the machine. The ancients, in the period we are considering, were not troubled by this question of freedom, because they did not think of Nature as a perfect machine.

That word 'machine' brings me to my third point: the question of the motive or driving impulse behind the two traditions of natural philosophy, the ancient and the modern. The difference in objective carries with it two different ways of looking at Nature. Scientific inquiry must select and concentrate attention upon certain aspects of the world, ignoring other aspects as irrelevant. And this selection is determined by interest, some feeling of need or desire, some value set upon this or that end in life.

Now it is a truism that the era of modern science with its mechanistic view of Nature has coincided with the era of mechanical invention, from Leonardo to Marconi. You will notice also that two of the later lectures in this series will deal with the relation of science to industry, in the Middle Ages and in modern times. But there is no lecture on the relation of ancient science to industry. The reason is that natural philosophy as pursued in the classical period had no bearing whatsoever on mechanical inventions. It was for this lack of interest in the means of production that the ancient philosophers were denounced in the first year of Queen Victoria by Lord Macaulay in his essay on Francis Bacon. Macaulay exalts Bacon as the apostle of modern scientific progress. A philosopher of our own day has recognised in Bacon the prophet of Big Business. There is surely some connection between the two descriptions. But listen for a moment to Macaulay's panegyric:

The chief peculiarity of Bacon's philosophy seems to us to have been this, that it aimed at things altogether different from those which his predecessors proposed to themselves. This was his own opinion.... What then was the end which Bacon proposed to himself? It was, to use his own emphatic expression, 'fruit'. It was the multiplying of human enjoyments and the mitigating of human sufferings....

Two words form the key of the Baconian doctrine, Utility and Progress. The ancient philosophy disdained to be useful and was content to be stationary....It could not condescend to the humble office of ministering to the comfort of human beings....Once indeed Posidonius, a distinguished writer of the age of Cicero and Caesar, so far forgot himself as to enumerate, among the humbler blessings which mankind owed to philosophy, the discovery of the principle of the arch, and the introduction of the use of metals....Seneca vehemently disclaims these insulting compliments. Philosophy, according to him, has nothing to do with teaching men to rear arched roofs over their heads. The true philosopher does not care whether he has an arched roof or any roof. Philosophy has nothing to do with teaching men the use of metals. She teaches us to be independent of all material substances, of all mechanical contrivances....

The ancient philosophers did not neglect natural science; but they did not cultivate it for the purpose of increasing the power and ameliorating the condition of man.... Seneca wrote largely on natural philosophy, and magnified the importance of that study. But why? Not because it tended to assuage suffering, to multiply the conveniences of life, to extend the empire of man over the material world; but solely because it tended to raise the mind above low cares, to separate it from the body, to exercise its subtilty in the solution of very obscure questions.

Finally, in a very eloquent passage, Macaulay rebukes the ancient philosophers for their failure to achieve the only practical good they aimed at: they did not 'form the minds of men to a high degree of wisdom or virtue'. Whereas no one can deny that nowadays every year makes an addition to what Bacon called 'fruit'. 'We know that guns, cutlery, spyglasses, clocks, are better in our time than they were in the time of our fathers, and were better in the time of our fathers than they were in the time of our grandfathers.'

It did not occur to Macaulay that a closely similar indictment might be drawn against the religion founded by one who said that man does not live by bread alone. But more recent disciples of the Baconian philosophy have not hesitated to accuse Christianity of failing to achieve its one practical aim: to make men love one another. Both failures must be frankly admitted. But no one, as Macaulay says, can deny that modern science has produced not only better cutlery and spyglasses, but better guns, to which we can now add incendiary bombs and poison gas.

Granting all this, as indeed we must, let us consider its bearing on our question of underlying motive. If the tree is to be known by its fruits, Macaulay's description of the Baconian fruits suggests that the conscious or unconscious aim of natural philosophy since the Renaissance has been to multiply the conveniences of life and to extend the empire of man over the material world—in a word, the increase of wealth and power. Certainly this was not the aim of natural philosophy in ancient times, which, accordingly, never tried to improve cutlery, guns, and spyglasses. And the difference of aim ought to throw light on those differences of method and objective which I have outlined.

That splendid and triumphant progress towards wealth and power, which has made Europe to-day so much happier than it was in the days of Pericles or of Marcus Aurelius, has been achieved by the invention of machines, which take the work out of human hands and perform it a thousand times more quickly and efficiently. And the construction of machine tools means enlisting the tremendous forces provided by Nature. The first forces to be utilized are the passive forces of weight and pressure exerted in the natural motions of air and water—the wind that fills the ship's sails, the stream that drives the water-wheel. It is significant that the pioneers of science in the sixteenth and seventeenth centuries, notably Galileo and Newton, were specially interested in the laws of motion and gravity, which they were the first to formulate. Later came the much more powerful active energy released by combustion. After taming earth and air and water, man harnessed fire to his engines of production.

You cannot effectively enlist these natural forces until you know a good deal of their working apart from human control. So a science ultimately bent on the fruits of power and wealth will find it useful to regard Nature itself as a machine of unsuspected complexity. The first task will be to take this machine to pieces, and to grasp the relation of one part to another, and how each part behaves. A machine must work with the greatest possible order and regularity. So the mechanical philosophy of Nature looks always for those invariable sequences of cause and effect which are the secret of its uniform behaviour. The results discovered are then transferred to machines contrived by human ingenuity. These machines will not work unless the behaviour of the forces employed has been apprehended correctly. Knowledge that is turned to practical use is constantly checked by results. Hence a whole technique of exact observation and cautious experiment will be invoked to make sure that the Jinn conjured out of the jar will serve the magician's will and not tear him to pieces.

Let us now contrast with this attitude towards Nature as a source of mechanical power the attitude of the ancient Atomists as formulated by Epicurus and reproduced by Lucretius. I take Epicurus for two reasons. First, Atomism has a closer kinship than any other ancient system with modern physics. Secondly, Macaulay saw in Epicureanism the one sect which ought not to have merited Bacon's condemnation. 'The Epicurean who referred all happiness to bodily pleasure and all evil to bodily pain might have been expected to exert himself for the purpose of bettering his own physical condition and that of his neighbours. But the thought never seems to have occurred to any member of that school.' True; but why was the Epicurean so indifferent?

It was, perhaps, not the fault of the philosophers that the ancients had so few machines driven by non-human force. The simple fact is that power for anything that could be called large-scale industry was then supplied by slaves—'living tools', as Aristotle called them. It is estimated that when Pericles died the population of Attica was divided into a little more than 200,000 freemen and 115,000 slaves. Abundant slave-labour makes it unnecessary to enlist non-human force in industry. There was thus no economic pressure driving men to study Nature as a source of mechanical power. The philosopher or man of science of any age, if he cares for knowledge and not for riches, has no personal motive to invent machinery for production. In a society where industry already has all the power it needs, you will not find the man of science installed in a factory, and devoting years of research to devising a process of making cotton fabrics that will not crease when folded.

But Epicurus was not merely free from any external pressure to discover the energy latent in his atoms. If he had held the key to unlock that energy and harness it to ever more powerful machines, then, like Prospero, he would have abjured that magic, and, deeper than did ever plummet sound, have drowned his book. He believed that human happiness depends, not on intense and varied pleasures, but on untroubled peace of mind; and that the pursuit of wealth and power had made man less happy even than his primitive ancestors before they found out the use of fire and the working of metals. As Lucretius says:

> If a man would order his life by a true principle, for him a frugal subsistence joined to a contented mind will be great riches; for he whose needs are small will never be in want. But men desired to be famous and powerful, hoping that their fortunes might rest on a firm foundation, and wealth might enable them to lead a tranquil life. But all in vain....
>
> Man labours to no purpose and wastes his life in fruitless cares, because he has not learnt what is the true end of possession, and up to what point true pleasure goes on increasing. This by slow degrees has carried life out into the deep sea, and stirred up from their lowest depths the mighty billows of war.

If my train of thought has been sound, this difference of motive and consequent interest—in the last resort a question of human values—lies at the root of the other differences we have noted. The arts of peace, as they were called in Macaulay's day, are now openly described in terms of the art of war. In Russia a party of labourers, who have painfully learnt what hard work means, are said to be despatched as 'shock troops' to 'the agricultural front'. All wars, as Plato remarked, are made for the purpose of getting money and the material things that money can buy. It is now admitted that industry at home and commerce abroad are a warfare waged for the same purpose. There is also the class war, to decide whether the money and the goods shall go to the rich or to the poor. I have suggested that, for economic reasons, the ancient study of Nature was not drawn into this perennial struggle. So it was suffered to remain as part of the pursuit of peaceful wisdom and of a happiness independent of wealth and even of material comfort. The fruits it gathered from the Tree of Knowledge were not the Baconian fruits of utility and progress.

A RITUAL BASIS FOR HESIOD'S
THEOGONY

PROFESSOR Mazon has recently described Hesiod's *Theogony* as 'a genealogy interrupted by episodes'. These episodes are myths, and Professor Mazon rightly remarks that their authenticity ought not to be suspected merely because they interrupt the genealogy, or because they are not consistent with one another. The texts produced by higher critics, who have given rein to such suspicions, leave the impression that the poem consists mainly of interpolations, like a bad sponge consisting mostly of holes. They are approaching the point at which the critics of the Pauline Epistles, having condemned them all, one after another, were left with no means of knowing what a genuine Pauline Epistle would be like. If the game was to go on, it was necessary to restore at least one to serve as a criterion for rejecting the remainder; and when that had been done, most of the others crept back again one by one into the canon.

This paper is inspired by the hope of rescuing some of the so-called episodes now jettisoned from the *Theogony*. I shall call in question what seems to be the current view, that the narrative parts of the poem are a mere patchwork of unconnected stories drawn from a variety of sources: Homer's account of the Olympian society; local cult-legends; other myths universally current in Greece; and a few stories too crudely indecent to be acknowledged as Hellenic.[1] I shall argue that the bulk of the episodes fit into the pattern of a very old myth of Creation, known to us from eastern sources and ultimately based on ritual.

Hesiod's own programme, laid down in the prelude, mentions three elements that are to figure in the poem: (1) theogony proper, i.e. the generations of the gods; (2) cosmogony, or the formation of the physical world-order and the creation of mankind; and (3) the story of how the gods took possession of

[1] So Ziegler in Roscher, *Lex. Myth.* s.v. 'Theogonien'.

Olympus under the supreme kingship of Zeus, who apportioned to the other gods their several provinces and honours.

(1) We can quickly pass over the first element—the genealogies of the gods. Hesiod gives three main lines of descent: (*a*) The children of Night prove to be a list of allegorical abstractions: Death, Sleep, the Fates, and all the afflictions which plague mankind. (*b*) The children of the Sea (Pontos), including a Dragon of the Waters with a brood of monsters, of whom we shall hear more later on. (*c*) Finally there are the offspring of Ouranos and Gaia: the earlier generation of Titans, Cyclopes, and the Hundred-Armed, and the second generation of the sons of Cronos, Zeus and the other Olympians and their descendants. These genealogies, though bewilderingly complicated, can be understood as an effort to combine in one pantheon a very miscellaneous collection of supernatural beings, ranging from the most concrete and anthropomorphic to the barest allegorical abstractions.

(2) Setting aside the genealogies, we come next to the second factor, cosmogony: 'how at the first the gods and earth came into being, and the rivers, and the swelling rage of the boundless sea, an: the shining stars, and the broad heaven above' (108-10). The cosmogony, so announced in the prelude, follows immediately. It is quite short, occupying seventeen lines of which three or four are possibly spurious (116–32).

We are here told how the main divisions of the existing cosmos came into being: the earth with its dry land and seas, and the sky above with its stars. The veil of mythological language is so thin as to be quite transparent. Ouranos and Gaia, for instance, are simply the sky and the earth that we see every day. They are not here supernatural persons with mythical biographies and adventures. Even when Earth is said to 'give birth' to the mountains and the sea, Hesiod himself tells us that this is conscious metaphor: a 'birth' can only follow upon a marriage, but here it occurs 'without love or marriage', ἄτερ φιλότητος ἐφιμέρου (132). The metaphor means no more than that this cosmogony is of the evolutionary type. There are no personal gods to make the world out of pre-existing materials according to the alternative pattern, the creational. The personal gods come later, when the world-order is already complete.

At that moment (132) Gaia and Ouranos suddenly become mythical persons, who marry and have children—Gaia is now a goddess, who can plot with her son Cronos to mutilate her husband Ouranos. We have passed into the world of myth, where the characters acquire the solidity and opaqueness of anthropomorphic individuals, with the whole apparatus of human motive and action.

(3) The remainder of the poem—the third of our three elements—moves in this genuine mythical atmosphere. It is a story of the adventures which led from the birth of the earliest gods to the final establishment of Zeus, triumphant over his enemies, as king of the gods and of the universe.

My object is to show that we have here not 'a genealogy interrupted by episodes', but a sequence of episodes, most of which once formed parts of a connected pattern, interrupted by genealogies, which serve to explain how the characters in the mythical action came into existence. The sequence of episodes itself constitutes what is, in essence, a hymn to Zeus and also a hymn of Creation—a mythical account of the beginning of things, immeasurably more primitive in character than the evolutionary cosmogony that precedes it. These two elements—the cosmogony and the hymn of Creation—are not in origin what Hesiod has made them, two chapters in a single story. The hymn is based on a genuine myth of enormous antiquity, itself founded on ritual. The cosmogony, on the other hand, has almost completely emerged from the atmosphere of myth. It is only just on the wrong side of the line we draw between mythical thinking and the earliest rational philosophy—the system of the Milesians.

CONTENTS OF THE COSMOGONY

Let us look first at the cosmogony.

I can only deal very shortly with its contents. I think it can be shown to conform to a pattern which also appears in the Orphic cosmogonies and underlies the Ionian systems of philosophy from Anaximander onwards.

(1) '*First of all Chaos came into being.*' There should be no doubt about the meaning of Chaos.[1] Etymologically, the word means a yawning gap; and in the Greek poets, including Hesiod himself (*Theog.* 700), it denotes the gap or void space between sky and earth. Bacchylides (v, 27) and Aristophanes (*Birds*, 192) speak of birds as flying in or through this space (διὰ τοῦ χάους, ἐν χάει).

A gap or yawn *comes into being* (Hesiod says γένετο, not ἦν) by the separation of two things that were formerly together. What these things were we learn from a fifth-century Ionian system, preserved by Diodorus (1, 7).[2] It opens with the words: 'Originally, heaven and earth had one form (μίαν ἰδέαν), their natures being mingled; then, when these bodies had taken up their stations apart from one another, the world embraced the whole order now seen in it.' Diodorus cites as parallel the famous lines of Euripides' Melanippe: 'The tale is not mine—I had it from my mother: how heaven and earth were once one form, and when they were separated apart, they gave birth to all things.'

Orpheus (Apollonius Rhodius, *Argon.* 1, 496) sang 'how earth and heaven and sea were once joined together in one form, and by deadly strife were separated from each other', then the heavenly bodies, mountains and rivers (dry land and water) were formed; and finally all living things.

Thus all these cosmogonies begin with a primal unity, which is separated apart, when the sky is lifted up from the earth, leaving the yawning gap of void or air between.

(2) By the opening of the gap, the broad bosom of Earth is revealed (γαῖα εὐρύστερνος), and Eros. Eros is an allegorical figure.

---

[1] Most modern discussions of this term are vitiated by the introduction of the later idea of infinite empty space, and by modern associations with disorder. I do not think Chaos is ever described as ἄπειρον, and if it were, that would mean no more than 'immeasurable', as when the word is used of the earth or the sea.

[2] This system is now ascribed (Diels-Kranz *Vors.*[5], II, 135) to Democritus; but there is no mention of atoms.

His function is to reunite the sundered parents, Heaven and Earth, in the marriage from which all life, mortal and immortal, is born. So we are told in the parabasis of the *Birds*: 'Before that there was no race of immortals, until Eros mixed all things together', συνέμειξεν: the use of μιγῆναι for marriage needs no illustration. Eros is the allegorical image of that intercourse of the separated opposites which will generate life.

His physical equivalent is the rain, the seed of the Heaven-father which fertilises the womb of mother Earth.

(3) Another physical consequence of the opening of the gap is that light is let in between the sundered parts. Accordingly we hear next of the appearance of light out of darkness. In genealogical terms, Darkness, as the male Erebos and the female Nyx, generates Light as the male Aither and the female Hemera. Day dawns from Night.

In one form of the Orphic cosmogony Eros is replaced by the spirit of light, Phanes, who appears when the world-egg is separated apart, the upper half forming the dome of heaven, the lower containing the moist slime from which the dry earth and the sea will emerge.

(4) The next event is startling. In spite of the fact that the gap separating heaven and earth has already come into being, we now hear that 'Earth first generated the starry heaven, equal to herself, to envelop her all round, that there might be for the blessed gods a seat secure for ever'.

Here is another separation of heaven from earth duplicating the opening of the gap. We shall soon encounter this duplication again, and when we get back to the original myth we shall be able to explain it.

Meanwhile let us note the epithet of heaven—'starry' (ἀστερόεις). This is expanded in Hesiod's proem: 'the shining stars of the broad heaven above' (110). Strange as it seems to us, the Ionian philosophers likewise regard the heavenly bodies as derived from the earth. They were explained mechanically as huge rocks, flung off to a distance, which became incandescent because of the speed of their motion.

(5) Then comes the distinction of the dry land from the sea: 'Earth gave birth to the high hills and to the sea (Pontos) with swelling waves.' This was *not* the result of a marriage, but ἄτερ φιλότητος ἐφιμέρου, another act of separation.

So again, in the Ionian systems, the last stage is the separation of dry from moist, when part of the earth is dried by the sun's heat, and the seas shrink into their beds.

The world-order is now complete as we see it, with its four great divisions: earth, sea, the gap of air, and starry sky above. From first to last the process is the separation or division, out of a primal indistinct unity, of parts which successively became distinct regions of the cosmos.

This cosmogony, as I have remarked, is not a myth, or rather it is *no longer* a myth. It has advanced so far along the road of rationalisation that only a very thin partition divides it from those early Greek systems which historians still innocently treat as purely rational constructions. Comparison with those systems shows that, when once the cosmic order has been formed, the next chapter should be an account of the origin of life. In the philosophies, life arises from the interaction or intercourse of the separated elements: animal life is born of the action of the heavenly heat on the moist slime of earth. This is the rationalised equivalent of the marriage of Heaven and Earth. And sure enough this marriage follows immediately in Hesiod: Gaia lay with Ouranos and brought forth the Titans. And so the genealogies begin—the theogony proper.

But here comes the sudden change I mentioned.

These gods are supernatural persons, with human forms and characters and well-known biographies. So at this point we turn back into that world of mythical representation which the rationalised cosmogony had left so far behind. Sky and Earth are re-transformed into a god and goddess, whose love and hate are depicted in all too human terms.

Here, where the mythical hymn to Zeus begins with the birth of the eldest gods, we must leave Hesiod for the moment to note a curiously close parallel to this sudden shift from rationalised cosmogony back to pure myth.

The first three chapters of Genesis contain two alternative accounts of Creation. The first account, in its present form, was composed not earlier than the Exile; it is considerably later than Hesiod, it may even be later than Anaximander. In this Hebrew cosmogony, moreover, we find nearly the same sequence of events. Let us recall what happened on the six days of Creation.

(1) There is the original confusion, the unformed watery mass wrapped in darkness. Light appears, divided from darkness, as day from night.

(So Hesiod's gap opened and Day was born from Night.)

(2) The sky as a solid firmament (στερέωμα) is lifted up to form a roof separating the heavenly waters, whence the rain comes, from the waters on the earth.

(This corresponds to Hesiod's Earth generating the sky as a secure seat for the gods. There is the same duplication that we noted.)

(3) The dry land is separated from the sea, and clothed with plants and trees.

(4) The heavenly bodies, sun, moon, and stars are made.

(As in the Greek myths and philosophies, their formation follows that of the earth.)

(5) & (6) Then came the moving creatures with life—birds, fishes, and creeping things—and finally man.

(Thus life appears when the cosmic frame is complete.)

The most striking difference from the Greek cosmogonies is that Hebrew monotheism has retained the Divine Creator as the sole first cause. Otherwise there are no mythical personifications, no allegorical figures like Eros or Phanes. And the action of the Elohim is confined to the utterance of the creative word. He has become extremely abstract and remote. If you eliminate the divine command: 'Let there be' so-and-so, and leave only the event commanded: 'There was' so-and-so, and then link these events in a chain of natural causation, the whole account is transformed into a quasi-scientific evolution of the world-order. The process is the same as in the Greek cosmogonies—separation or differentiation out of a primitive confusion. And as measured by the absence of allegorical personifications, Genesis is less mythical than Hesiod's *Theogony*, and even closer to the rationalised system of the Milesians.

When we turn to the second account of Creation in Genesis ii-iii, we find ourselves back once more in the world of myth. The utterly remote Elohim of the first chapter is replaced by an anthropomorphic Jahweh, who moulds man out of dust, breathes life into his nostrils, plants a garden with trees, takes the man's rib and makes out of it a woman, walks in the garden in the cool of the day, and speaks to Adam with a human voice. The substance of the story also is composed of genuine myths: the woman Eve and the trouble she brings recall Hesiod's Pandora; there is the myth explaining man's mortality by failure to eat the fruit of the tree of life; and so on.

These myths may represent the concluding episodes in a primitive Creation myth. The earlier part, dealing with the formation of the world-order before man was made, has been suppressed by the priestly compilers of Genesis. They substituted for it their own expurgated and semi-philosophical cosmogony in the first chapter.

There is thus a curious parallel between Hesiod and Genesis. In both we find a prosaic cosmogony followed by a shift back into the world of poetry, peopled by the concrete human figures of mythical gods. This is no mere accident. In each case the cosmogony is the final product of a long process of rationalisation, in which the expurgation of mythical imagery has been carried so far that the result might almost be mistaken for a construction of the intellect reasoning from observation of the existing world. Only when we reflect on certain features do we realise that it can be nothing of the kind. There is nothing whatever in the obvious appearance of the world to suggest that the sky ever had to be lifted up from the earth, or that the heavenly bodies were formed after the earth, and so on. The same remark applies to the slightly more rationalised cosmogonies of the Ionian philosophers. They follow the same pattern, which pattern could never have been designed by inference from the observation of nature.

Now the value of the parallel I have drawn with Hebrew cosmogony lies in the fact that the Old Testament has preserved elsewhere other traces of the original myth of Creation which the priestly authors of Genesis have largely obliterated. This myth has been restored by scholars, and, what is more, traced to its origin in ritual. And behind this Palestinian myth and ritual lie the Babylonian Hymn of Creation and the corresponding New Year rites. If we follow this track, we shall, I believe, discover the framework of those episodes which make up the third element in Hesiod's *Theogony*—the mythical hymn to Zeus.

THE OPENING OF CHAOS

We may start from that curious feature I have emphasised: the fact that, both in Hesiod and Genesis, the separation of sky from earth occurs twice over. We will take the two versions of this event separately.

First there is the opening of the gap and the appearance of light in the primaeval darkness. Turning from Hesiod's cosmogony to the hymn which follows, we find that this event has its counterpart in the first episode of the myth. Fifty years ago Andrew Lang pointed out that the mutilation of the sky-god by his son Cronos could be 'explained as a myth of the violent separation of the earth and sky, which some races, for example the Polynesians, supposed to have originally clasped each other in a close embrace'. I quote these words from Frazer's *Adonis* (I, 283); and this explanation is adopted by Nilsson in his *History of Greek Religion* (p. 73).

After mentioning the Orphic world-egg, Nilsson writes: 'Still more crude is the cosmogonic myth in Hesiod. Ouranos (the sky) settled down upon Gaia (the earth), completely covering her, and hid their children in her entrails. Gaia persuaded her son Kronos to part them by cutting off the genitalia of Ouranos. There are curious parallels in the Egyptian myth of Keb and Nut, the earth-god and the goddess of heaven, and in the Maori myth of Rangi and Papa.'

In this myth we read: [1] 'From Rangi, the Heaven, and Papa, the Earth, sprang all men and things; but sky and earth clave together,

[1] Tylor, *Primitive Culture* I, 322.

and darkness rested upon them and the beings they had begotten, till at last their children took counsel whether they should rend apart their parents or slay them.'

Tane Mahute separated them and raised up the sky. The gods then departed each to his separate place in air, earth, and sea, and thus the world was established. We may note further that as, in Hesiod's Cosmogony, the opening of the gap is followed by the appearance of Eros, so in his myth the sundering of Ouranos and Gaia is followed by the birth of Aphrodite, who has Eros and Himeros in her train and whose prerogative (τιμή and μοῖρα) is to preside over marriage (201–6).

The Polynesian myth brings out more clearly than Hesiod does the purpose for which heaven and earth were forced apart: it was to give the gods room in which to be born and distinct regions they could occupy in a world-order. In the language of myth, it enables Gaia to give birth to her children, Pontos and the other gods. In the language of rationalised cosmogony, it is followed by the separation of the sea from the dry land and the appearance of living things. Once you have granted the fundamental axiom that 'heaven and earth were once one form' (or, as the philosophers put it, 'all things were together', ἦν ὁμοῦ πάντα), theogony and cosmogony alike must begin with the separation of the two parents of the gods or the two primary regions of the cosmos.

The agent in the mythical version is Cronos, instigated by Gaia herself. To that extent Cronos fills the role of creator. Also he was the king, who originally distributed among the Titans their privileges and provinces in the order of the world (*Theog.* 392 ff.). But his reign has receded into the dim past. In the hymn the foreground is occupied by his son, the young king, Zeus. Zeus is the hero whose exploits established the world as it now is.

THE DRAGON

So much, then, for the original opening of the gap. We will now go on to the second version of this act of separation. In Hesiod, Earth gives birth to the heaven and the shining stars. In Genesis, Elohim lifts up the firmament to support the heavenly ocean and creates the sun, moon, and stars. What is the mythical counterpart of this episode in cosmogony?

Once more the answer is to be found in the pages of the *Golden Bough*. Frazer writes:

> The Babylonian myth relates how in the beginning the mighty god Marduk fought and killed the great dragon Tiamat, an embodiment of the primaeval watery chaos, and how after his victory he created the present heaven and earth by splitting the huge carcase of the monster into halves and setting one of them up to form the sky, while the other half apparently he used to fashion the earth. Thus the story is a myth of creation.... The account of creation given in the first chapter of Genesis, which has been so much praised for its simple grandeur and sublimity, is merely a rationalised version of the old myth of the fight with the dragon, a myth which for crudity of thought deserves to rank with the quaint fancies of the lowest savages.[1]

Frazer is referring to the Babylonian so-called 'Epic of Creation'. We there read how Tiamat the dragon of the waters, seeking vengeance on the younger gods for killing her husband Apsu, organised a host of monsters. She defeats the first champion of the gods, who then appeal to Marduk. He undertakes to save them, if he is promised kingship over the whole world. Exalted as a great god, he kills the dragon and imprisons her monsters in the lower world. He then splits her body in half to make sky and earth; fixes the regions of the world-order, and assigns the three provinces of heaven, earth, and sea to Anu, Enlil, and Ea. He orders the year and the signs of the Zodiac and other heavenly bodies. There is a long description of the constellations.

Here we have, in its oldest known form, the lifting-up of the starry heaven from the earth followed by the ordering of the stars and of the provinces in the cosmos. We have seen how all this is rationalised in Genesis i and reduced to the formation of the firmament, the creation of the heavenly bodies, the separation of land and sea.

Now the link connecting the Babylonian myth with Genesis i is provided by references in the Psalms and Prophets to the myth

[1] *The Dying God*, p. 105.

of Jahweh slaying the dragon Rahab or Leviathan. Here is one of many:

> God is my king of old, working salvation in the midst of the earth.
> Thou didst divide the sea by thy strength; thou brakest the heads of the dragons in the waters.
> Thou breakest the heads of leviathan in pieces....
> The day is thine, the night also is thine; thou hast prepared the light and the sun.
> Thou hast set all the borders of the earth: thou hast made summer and winter.[1]

Here the dividing of the waters by the firmament is equated with the breaking of the dragon in pieces. It is followed by the creation of light and the sun, the ordering of the seasons, and fixing of the borders of the earth.

Now in Hesiod, one of the most exciting episodes is the slaying of the dragon by Zeus. This is one of the passages which the editors condemn on account of some inconsistency and dislocation. Among the descendants of Pontos we find the half-human dragon Echidna, who in marriage with Typhaon produces a brood of monsters (*Theog.* 295 ff.). Later (820), after the expulsion of the Titans from heaven, comes the battle of Zeus with the dragon Typhoeus, here the child of Earth and Tartarus. The whole of nature is involved in the turmoil of this terrific struggle. After his victory, Zeus, like Marduk, is established as king over the gods, and apportions to them their stations in the world-order.

On the strength of the Hebrew and Babylonian parallels (not to mention others), I claim that the battle of Zeus and the dragon Typhoeus is an original feature of the Greek Creation myth, which should be followed by the lifting up of the sky and the formation of the heavenly bodies. Of this sequel just a trace remains in the cosmogony, where the earth gives birth to the heaven and the shining stars—the second of those two separations of heaven and earth which we have noted.

It is now possible to explain why this separation occurs twice.

[1] Ps. lxxiv. 12-17.

In the rationalised cosmogonies it is inexplicable; but the reason appears in the myth. There the work of creation is the exploit of a personal god—Marduk, Jahweh, Zeus—who can bring light out of darkness, order out of formlessness, only by first triumphing over the powers of evil and disorder embodied in the dragon of the waters and her brood of monsters.[1] But this exploit must happen *somewhere*: the drama requires a stage. Also the hero must have a birth and history; and if he is to be the son of Heaven and Earth, his parents must have become distinct before they could marry and have a child.

Hence the necessity that the whole story should begin with the gap coming into being. In Hesiod's cosmogony, this simply happens: the first event has no cause behind it. But in myth all events are apt to have personal causes. So we find that Ouranos and Gaia are forced apart by Cronos, before the gods can be born, including Zeus himself. The result is this curious duplication. Heaven and earth are first separated in order to give birth to the god, who will create the world by separating heaven from earth as the two parts of the dragon.

But it is high time for me to fulfil the promise of my title which suggests that Hesiod's *Theogony* is, in the last resort, based on ritual. So far I have only argued that his all-but philosophical cosmogony is a rational reflection of his mythical hymn of Zeus, just as Genesis i is a reflection of the myths of Jahweh and Marduk. But I have only dealt with two episodes in the myth. In the light of the oriental material we can now go further and ask whether other episodes in the hymn of Zeus will not fit into a connected pattern, and whether this pattern may not be referred ultimately to a sequence of ritual acts.

It is now certainly established that the killing of Leviathan by Jahweh or of Tiamat by Marduk was not what Frazer called a 'quaint fancy' of primitive and problematical savages, sitting round the fire and speculating on the origin of the world. Nor was this conflict an isolated event without a context. Biblical

---

[1] Roscher, *Lex*. s.v. 'Ophion'. Jensen suggested that the battle of Χρόνος-Κρόνος with Ophioneus in Pherecydes' cosmogony is equivalent to the battle of Marduk and Tiamat.

students[1] have made out that the Psalms celebrating it belong to a group of liturgical songs, which were recited, as part of the Temple worship, at the Feast of Tabernacles. This feast inaugurated the New Year; and in its dramatic ritual the events these Psalms describe were annually re-enacted.

It is inferred from the Psalms that the fight with the dragon was one episode in the drama, in which, as throughout the festival, the part of Jahweh was taken by the king. There was also a triumphal procession, conducting the divine king in his chariot up the hill of Zion to be enthroned in the temple. Emblems of new vegetation, fertility, and moisture were carried and waved as a charm to secure a sufficiency of rain for the coming year. There are also signs that, at some point in the king's progress, there was another ritual combat. The procession was assailed by the powers of darkness and death, who are also the enemies of Israel, the kings of the earth who took counsel together against the Lord's anointed. The god who wields the thunder intervened to save his royal son and to dash his enemies in pieces. This episode has a parallel in the annual ritual at Abydos in Egypt. The procession conducting Osiris to his shrine was attacked by a band representing Set and his followers, who were repelled by a company led by Horus. At Jerusalem there was probably also a sacred marriage in a grove, commemorated by the booths made of branches from which the festival took its name, Tabernacles.

It appears, then, that the slaying of the dragon by the king-god, which was the initial act of creation, was one feature in the dramatic ritual of the New Year festival. What is the connection between a New Year festival and the myth of Creation?

This question has been convincingly answered by oriental scholars. The festival was much more than the civic inauguration of another year. It was in the first place a ceremony whose magical efficacy was to secure, during the coming year, the due supply of rain and the consequent fertility of plants and animals, on which man's life depends. This purpose was never forgotten. It is stated in the simplest terms by the prophet Zechariah (xiv. 16), who

---

[1] Prof. W. O. E. Oesterley in *Myth and Ritual*, chap. VI; A. R. Johnson in *The Labyrinth*.

foretells that, when the Lord is King over the whole earth, every one that is left of all the nations which came against Jerusalem shall go up from year to year to worship the King, the Lord of Hosts, and to keep the feast of Tabernacles—'And it shall be, that whoso will not come up...*upon them shall be no rain*.'

So the central figure in the New Year rites was the rain-maker, the divine king. But at the advanced stage of civilisation we are now considering in Babylon, Egypt, and Palestine, the king has become much more than a rain-making magician. To control the rain is to control the procession of the seasons and their powers of drought and moisture, heat and cold; and these again are linked with the orderly revolutions of sun, moon, and stars. The king is thus regarded as the living embodiment of the god who instituted this natural order and must perpetually renew and maintain its functioning for the benefit of man. The king embodies that power and also the life-force of his people, concentrated in his official person. He is the maintainer of the social order; and the prosperity of the nation depends upon his righteousness, the Hebrew *Sedek*, the Greek δίκη. He protects his people from the evil powers of death and disorder, as well as leading them in war to victory over their enemies.

The purpose of the New Year festival is to renovate—to recreate—the ordered life of the social group and of the world of nature, after the darkness and defeat of winter. The power which gives one more turn to the wheel of the revolving year is vested in the king, but derived from the god whom he embodies, the god who first set the wheel in motion. So the rites are regarded as an annual re-enactment of Creation.

Commenting on the features common to the New Year festivals of Babylon and Egypt, Professor Oesterley remarks [1] that, while there are many gods,

there is one who assumes supremacy in the role of productive creator; and the earthly king is identified with him. Osiris among the Egyptians, and Marduk among the Babylonians, are the supreme gods, and in each case the earthly king is identified with his god. During the annual New Year Festival held in honour of the deity he is proclaimed king;

[1] *Myth and Ritual*, p. 123.

and this is graphically set forth in the drama of his ascent upon his throne; he is thereby acknowledged as lord of creation. The mystery-rite not only symbolised, but was believed actually to bring about, the revivification of Nature.

Now, what Osiris was to the Egyptians, and what Marduk was to the Babylonians, that Jahweh was to the Israelites. The New Year Festival of the Israelites was held on the first day of the Feast of Tabernacles (Sukkoth), when the Kingship of their God Jahweh was celebrated, and he was worshipped and honoured as Lord of Creation. By his will...the produce of the soil during the coming year would be abundant; thus, annually there was the renewed manifestation of His creative power, so that every New Year Festival was a memorial of the Creation, since at each New Year the land was recreated....It may be said that the New Year Festival was, as it were, a repetition of the Creation.

To the same effect Professor Hooke has written of the Babylonian ceremony:

It was, in a literal sense, the making of a New Year, the removal of the guilt and defilement of the old year, and the ensuring of security and prosperity for the coming year. By this ceremony was secured the due functioning of all things, sun, moon, stars, and seasons, in their appointed order. Here lies the ritual meaning of Creation: there is a new creation year by year, as a result of these ceremonies. The conception of creation in this stage of the evolution of religion is not cosmological but ritual. It has not come into existence in answer to speculations about the origin of things, but as a ritual means of maintaining the necessary order of things essential for the well-being of the community.[1]

We can now define the relation between the Creation myth and the New Year rites. It is the relation called 'aetiological'. Here the Babylonian evidence is conclusive. We possess a large part of the myth in the tablets now misleadingly entitled 'The Epic of Creation'. This is not an epic, but a hymn. Epics do not reflect ritual action; nor were they recited as incantations to reinforce the efficacy of a rite every time it was performed. This document is a hymn to Marduk, recounting his exploits in creating and ordering the world of gods and men.

[1] *Origins of Early Semitic Ritual*, p. 19.

We know, moreover, that, on the fourth day of the New Year festival of the spring equinox, this hymn was recited, from beginning to end, by the high priest, shut up alone in the sanctuary. This was done before the king arrived to take the leading part in the principal ceremonies.

Further, fragments of a priestly commentary on the ritual explain that a whole series of actions performed by the king symbolised the exploits of Marduk in the story of Creation. That story is, in fact, the aetiological myth of the New Year festival.

Now we know that an aetiological myth is not really the historical record of a supernatural series of events instituting the rite which professes to re-enact these events on a miniature scale. The rite itself is the only historical event, repeated annually. Every spring the king-god actually recreates the natural and social order. The myth is a transcription of that performance on a higher plane, where the corresponding actions are imagined as performed once for all by the god whom the king is conceived to embody and represent. But that god is simply a projection, made up of the official character and functions of the king, abstracted from the accidental human personality who is invested with those functions so long as his vitality lasts in full vigour. When he grows old or dies, the divine character is transmitted to a successor. The god is related to the individual king as the Platonic Idea to a series of particulars which for a time manifest its character. The myth is similarly the universalised transcript of the recurrent ritual action, projected on to the superhuman plane.

It follows that the contents of the Creation myth are not 'quaint fancies', or baseless speculations; nor are they derived from the observation of natural phenomena. Starting from the given appearance of the starry sky above our heads and the broad earth at our feet, no one but a lunatic under the influence of hashish could ever arrive at the theory that they were originally formed by splitting the body of a dragon in half. But suppose you start with a ritual drama, in which the powers of evil and disorder, represented by a priestly actor with a dragon's mask, are overcome by the divine king, as part of a magical regeneration of the natural and social order. Then you may compose a hymn, in which this act is magnified, with every circumstance of splendour and horror, as a terrific battle between the king of the gods and the dragon of the deep. And you will recite this hymn, every time the ritual drama is performed, to reinforce its efficacy with all the majesty of the superhuman precedent.

Now so long as the myth remains part of a living ritual, its symbolic meaning is clear. But when the ritual has fallen into disuse, the myth may survive for many centuries. The action will now appear crude, grotesque, monstrous; and yet a poet may instinctively feel that the story is still charged with significance, however obscure, owing to the intense emotions that went to its making when it was part of vitally important religious action. Symbols like the dragon still haunt the dreams of our most civilised contemporaries.

The suggestion, then, to which all this intricate argument has led, is that the mythical element in the *Theogony* consists mainly in the debris of a Creation myth which is also a hymn to Zeus. By Hesiod's time it had long been detached from the ritual it once reflected, and the episodes have naturally suffered some dislocation. Also, since Hesiod was unaware of the ritual origin which alone makes them intelligible, the outlines are sometimes blurred. But if we pass them briefly in review, the ancient pattern can still be traced.

(1) Hesiod's myth is linked with the preceding cosmogony by the marriage of Ouranos and Gaia, parents of the elder gods; the Cyclopes, who will furnish Zeus with his thunder; the Hundred-Armed, who will fight for him against the Titans; and the Titans themselves.

Ouranos hates his children, who cannot get born until Cronos castrates his father and forces the pair apart.

In the Babylonian myth the first parents are the male and female powers of the primaeval deep, Apsu and Tiamat, whose waters at first were mingled together. Apsu wishes to destroy his children, the elder gods. Ea plots against Apsu, kills him, and castrates his messenger, Mummu.

(2) Here follow in Hesiod three genealogies. The children of Night include Death and all the evils that plague mankind.

Among the descendants of Pontos is the dragon Echidna with her consort Typhaon and their brood of monsters.

In the Babylonian hymn, Tiamat plans to avenge Apsu, with the help of monsters born of the sea. She exalts Kingu among her first-born to be king over her other children, much as Gaia chose Cronos to take the lead among the Titans.

(3) Both poems then tell of the birth of the young God—Marduk, Zeus—who is to become king and order the world of men and gods.

This part of the story of Zeus is of Cretan origin. Once more the old king tries to destroy his sons who will rob him of his kingship, and is defeated by a stratagem.

It will be remembered how in the Palaikastro hymn the fertility aspect of the young Zeus appears when he leads the dancing Kouretes, and is invoked to bring fruitfulness for the coming year.

In Hesiod Zeus releases the Hundred-Armed and the Cyclopes, who give him the thunder that will assure his kingship.

As Nilsson remarks, a fertility god who is annually reborn must also die annually. The death of Zeus was a part of the Cretan myth which the Greeks suppressed.

It is noteworthy that the death of Marduk does not figure in the Creation myth; but we possess tablets recording the ritual of his death and resurrection, which somehow accompanied the New Year festival. The ritual resembled that of Tammuz; and, while Bel-Marduk was in the underworld, the hymn of Creation was sung as an incantation to secure his return to life.

(4) Hesiod's story is here interrupted by the genealogy of Iapetos, which leads to the cheating of Zeus by Prometheus, the theft of fire, and the creation of woman to plague mankind. These events, which imply that man has already been created, are obviously out of place. At line 617 Hesiod goes back to the release of the Hundred-Armed. Zeus gives them the food of immortality, and they undertake to fight the Titans, who are attacking Olympus. The battle is indecisive until Zeus, now armed with the thunder, intervenes. The Titans are blasted and imprisoned in Tartarus.

These Titans who assail Olympus can hardly be the same as the children of Ouranos called Titans in the earlier genealogy. We cannot believe that the lovely Tethys, the gold-crowned Phebe, and two brides of Zeus, Themis and Mnemosyne, can have been battered with rocks, blasted by the lightning, and permanently chained in Tartarus.

This story has grown out of the ritual combat in which the forces of death and disorder, the followers of Set, the kings of the earth, attack the company of the young king, and are defeated by the god whom he represents. If this is so, the Titanomachy perpetuates a feature of New Year ritual.

(5) In the Babylonian myth the enemies of the younger gods are Tiamat and her host of monsters. She defeats their first champion, Anu. The gods then appeal to Marduk, who undertakes to save them if he is promised kingship over the whole world. The gods do homage to him and invest him with the insignia of royalty. There is a terrific battle, told at great length. Tiamat is slain and her monsters imprisoned.

Marduk then splits her body to make heaven and earth, fixes the regions of the world-order, and assigns heaven, earth, and sea to Anu, Enlil, and Ea as their provinces. (Compare the δασμός of these same regions to the three sons of Cronos.)

Marduk orders the year, the signs of the Zodiac, and the other heavenly bodies.

Man is created by Ea from the blood of Tiamat's consort, Kingu.

Marduk then gives laws to the gods and fixes their prerogatives. In gratitude, they build the temple of E-Sagila, where they assemble every year for the New Year festival—that very festival of which this hymn reflects the ritual.

In Hesiod the battle with the dragon Typhoeus comes after the expulsion of the Titans, as the last exploit of Zeus. It cannot be followed by the work of Creation, since the formation of the world-order has already been described in the cosmogony prefixed to the whole myth and Hesiod is too logical to repeat it here. But it is followed by the final recognition of Zeus as king over the gods, to whom he apportions their prerogatives.

Thus Zeus institutes the natural and social order. This royal function is allegorically expressed by the marriage of Zeus with

Themis (social order) and the birth of their children, the Seasons (whose names are Good Government, Justice, and Peace) and the Moirai, who give men their portions of good and evil.

So the last event in the hymn of Marduk is that the seven gods of fate fix the destinies for all mankind.

The parallel I have drawn might be illustrated in much greater detail. But perhaps there is now a *prima facie* case for the thesis that Hesiod's hymn of Zeus is not a genealogy interrupted by unconnected episodes, but reflects the features of an ancient New Year ritual of recreation, in which the king impersonated Zeus. The myth may have been for a long time detached from the ritual. Hesiod cannot have been aware of its origin; but he must have been dimly conscious that just these episodes were relevant to the story of Creation. Further research in Crete and Asia Minor may show whether there is any ground for the guess that the New Year festival in question was once performed in the palace of King Minos.

NOTE

The following is added at the end of the MS. of this essay, with a note saying that it was occasioned by a criticism of Prof. A. B. Cook to the effect that it ought to be possible to point to a ritual *on Greek soil*, of which the myth discussed might be the aetiology.   W. K. C. G.

I am wondering whether this New Year festival is not the original parent of a lot of festivals, including the Dionysia (New Year festivals need not be in spring), which have diverged by emphasising different features of the original until they may seem to have as little in common as a horse's leg, the human forearm and hand, and a bird's wing. Thus the death and resurrection element may be almost entirely suppressed in one form (as at Babylon, where it survived only as an extraneous rite and in the humiliation of the divine king by the high priest, of which there is a trace still in the coronation rite). Elsewhere this feature might become central and all-important: then you have the ritual which yields tragedy and comedy. Hocart's *Kingship* suggests that you might derive from the one source also the coronation ritual and the initiation ceremonies of Eleusinian type (which were agricultural-fertility rites, *not* tribal initiations). In Osiris's case the death and resurrection *motif* is central, but other features survive.

There is only one fundamental theme behind all these: renewal of life; rebirth; the young king superseding the old.

What excited me was the idea (which I got from Hooke's books) that early philosophic cosmogony is not only a transcription of mythical cosmogony, but finally has its root in *ritual*, something tangibly existing, not baseless 'fancies' and speculation.

THE MARXIST VIEW OF ANCIENT PHILOSOPHY

THE subject of this paper is the application of the Marxist interpretation of history to ancient philosophy in two recent books: Mr Farrington's *Science and Politics in the Ancient World* and Mr George Thomson's *Aeschylus and Athens*. Mr Thomson's book covers a much wider field; his references to the philosophers are only incidental. But he seems to share Mr Farrington's view of them; and he is an avowed believer in the Marxist doctrine.

A word must first be said about this doctrine. I will quote one statement of it from a work which is still cited as authoritative.

Engels, in his polemic against the unfortunate Dühring,[1] declared that the conception of history had been decisively changed by the 'new facts' of the working-class movements in the 1830's and 1840's. 'The new facts', he says, 'made imperative a new examination of all past history, and then it was seen that *all* past history was the history of class struggles, that these warring classes of society are always the product of the modes of production and exchange, in a word of the *economic* conditions of their time; that therefore the economic structure of society always forms the real basis from which, in the last analysis, is to be explained the whole superstructure of legal and political institutions, as well as the religious, philosophical, and other conceptions of each historical period. Now idealism was driven from its last refuge, the philosophy of history; now a materialist conception of history was propounded, and the way found to explain man's conciousness by his being, instead of, as heretofore, his being by his consciousness.'

This is a very sweeping statement. I shall try to follow out its implications in a train of thought which can be traced in Mr Farrington's treatment of the history of philosophy, and in particular in his view of Epicurus and Plato.

[1] *Anti-Dühring* (English trans.), p. 32.

I am not at all concerned to deny that the economic interpretation of history has thrown into relief certain neglected factors which have had some influence on the course of religious and philosophic speculation. I have long believed that at least some philosophic and scientific concepts have a social origin, in one sense of that highly ambiguous phrase. In a book published thirty years ago I tried to trace some of them back to collective representations current in pre-scientific ages and preserved in later myth and poetry. But at that time I had never heard of dialectical materialism, and my speculations (for what they were worth) were entirely independent of Marxian doctrine. Now that I have made some study of that doctrine, I can see further light to be gained from that quarter. The history of philosophy may be brought into closer touch with the history of other forms of human activity, provided that the influence of economic and other social factors can be measured and appraised dispassionately.

But here at once—over that word 'dispassionately'—I find myself at issue with my Marxian friends. They will not admit that either the philosophers themselves, or the scholar who interprets them, can be dispassionate or disinterested. For the Marxian there can be no light without heat; indeed the more light he sees, the hotter he becomes.

The reason appears plainly in that passage I quoted from Engels. The Marxian doctrine took shape a century ago, when the Industrial Revolution had produced an acute crisis in the class-war, and Europe seemed to be in the birth-throes of a social revolution, which proved to be abortive. The Communist Manifesto was issued in 1848; and since then it has become the fighting creed of a very energetic political party. The members of such a party find strength in the conviction that their opponents, even in the sphere of abstract thought and scholarship, are not merely mistaken, but selfishly clinging to their wealth and social position. Their own generous sympathy with the oppressed is further strengthened by an interpretation of all history which assures them that they are on the right side, that is to say, on the side which is bound to win. If they even tried to be dispassionate, their attitude would be worse than wrong: it would be 'unhistorical'.

Fortified by this creed, the Marxian carries back into the study of the past that mood of righteous indignation which is so appropriate to a partisan in the contemporary conflict. Quite naturally; since he holds that 'all past history is the history of class struggles', and all philosophical systems are reflections, on the plane of abstract ideas, of the economic antagonisms of society. It follows that the philosophers, and even the poets in so far as they have philosophies of life, must be lined up on one or the other side of the class conflict, as it was being waged in the society of their time and place. Their professedly disinterested speculations must be correlated with some economic or social change. Those who can be ranged on the side of the social forces which were in fact destined to prevail, will be approved as revolutionary and progressive. Those who appear to be supporting a cause which was in fact destined to be lost, will be denounced as selfishly trying to perpetuate the privileges of their own class. Now, if we approach the study of Greek philosophy from this angle, we notice at once that (as the ancients themselves perceived) there were two main traditions running side by side all the way through. At various points, indeed, they might overlap and flow into one another in composite systems; but on the whole they maintained a distinct character, and, as time went on, came into more open conflict.

The first tradition was called Ionian. Starting from Thales and Anaximander, it was continued in the fifth century by Anaxagoras, Archelaus, Diogenes of Apollonia, and found its most fortunate expression in the Atomism of Democritus, adopted and modified by Epicurus. The trend of this tradition was towards materialism— the belief that reality is to be found in the bodies we can see and handle, and that the soul consists merely of bodies of specially fine texture, destined to be dispersed at the moment of death. The existence of gods was not denied; but they were not to interfere with the course of physical events, which is left to the purposeless play of necessity and chance.

The other tradition, called Italian, starts from Pythagoras. It throws the emphasis, not on matter, but on form, and sets the interests of an immortal soul above those of the perishable body. It culminates in the Platonic idealism, which asserts that soul is ontologically prior to body and is the source of all bodily motion. Reality is immaterial, accessible to thought, but not to the senses. The shifting world of appearances can yield no certain knowledge. Although its main structure shows evidence of intelligent design, there is, strictly speaking, no science of nature, because the rational principle of order in the universe has not completely prevailed over that unruly element of chance and necessity, which holds undisputed sway in the Ionian systems.

Confronted with these two traditions, there is no doubt where the sympathy of the Marxian will lie. His materialist interpretation of history, itself a reaction against the idealist interpretation of Hegel, is bound up with materialism in the philosophic sense. Having laid down that all religious and philosophical conceptions are ultimately traceable to economic relations and modes of production of material goods, he naturally embraces the doctrine that matter is primary and actually existed before mind, while mind and all its creations are somehow a secondary superstructure, or reflection, or epiphenomenon. And when he speaks of matter, he is thinking, I suspect, of something much more like the solid atoms of Epicurus or of Sir Isaac Newton [1] than like anything that the physics of the twentieth century would recognise as existent. Accordingly, he will favour the Ionian strand in Greek thought, as against the Platonic.

We are now prepared to find Mr Farrington upholding the Ionian philosophy, and above all the atomism of Epicurus, on three grounds: first, as scientifically true, so far as it went; secondly, as potentially useful for material progress; and thirdly, as philanthropic in another sense—a popular philosophy, promising to emancipate the 'little people' from the tyranny of oligarchs like Plato, who wished to hold them in permanent subjection by denying them access to truth and poisoning their minds with outworn superstitions.

I propose to take these three points separately, and to explain briefly why this picture seems to me to distort the facts.

[1] Newton described atoms as 'solid, massy, hard, impenetrable particles... even so hard as never to wear or break in pieces' (quoted by Dampier, *A History of Science*, 4th ed. p. 170).

(1) First, there is the question of scientific truth. Can it be claimed for any of the Ionian systems, from Anaximander to Epicurus, that they were solidly based on grounds which any candid inquirer would be bound to accept?

Mr Farrington opens his account of the Ionians by asserting, as 'a fact which anyone can confirm', that 'the kind of things that Anaximander was saying in his book *On Nature* were the same kind of things that an up-to-date writer puts forward to-day in a scientific handbook of the universe'.[1] He then gives an outline of Anaximander's system in modern terms, omitting its archaic features, and so incidentally obliterating all traces of those social origins which Mr Thomson has rightly emphasised. Finally, Mr Farrington tells us that Anaximander knew that he had arrived, 'by looking at the universe about him and thinking about what he saw' (i.e., by observation and reflection), at a new kind of knowledge, which he thought 'could be trusted to make its way by itself with intelligent people, and would be found useful to humanity'.

This statement, no doubt, represents part of the truth; but it fails to account for those features which Mr Farrington omits. What sort of observation could have taught Anaximander that the earth is a cylindrical drum, three times as broad as it is high; or that the fixed stars, the moon, and the sun, in that order, are respectively distant from the earth by 9, 18, and 27 times the diameter of the earth? Yet he made these assertions with the same dogmatic confidence as all the rest. These are *not* the same kind of things that we find in up-to-date scientific handbooks, because the modern man of science is restrained by a conception of scientific method of which none of these Ionians had any inkling.

All the Ionian systems were, in fact, chiefly concerned with matters beyond the reach of observation. They speculated about the way in which an ordered world might have arisen from some sort of chaos; about the ultimate constituents of material bodies; and about the possible origin of life, on the assumption that life was not supernaturally created.

If we take Anaximander's cosmogony with all its archaic

[1] Op. cit. p. 19.

features, it can, I believe, be shown to be a rationalisation of an ancient Creation myth. The social origin of his philosophy is to be found there, not in the economic conditions of sixth-century Miletus. He inherited from mythical thought a scheme of cosmogony in which the operating factors had originally been conceived as personal gods. Expurgating the factors he could recognise as mythical, he substituted for the gods the operation of powers, such as 'the hot' and 'the cold', which he took to be unquestionably natural. But he kept the fundamental framework of the myth. The structure of his system was not the outcome of unbiased reflection on observed phenomena.

This work of rationalising expurgation was, of course, a very remarkable step towards what we call natural science. But it was, in essence, a dogmatic speculation, with no more claim to have established truth on grounds which any intelligent person must accept than had any of the other Ionian systems which followed.

This remark holds good of atomism, a theory which was not inferred from observation, but derived from the earlier Pythagorean doctrine that all things are made of 'numbers'—numbers conceived in a material fashion, as both geometrical points and indivisible units of which bodies consist. That doctrine had given rise to a logical and mathematical debate, carried on by the Eleatics, who denied the real existence of plurality and change. The atomism of Democritus was an expedient to restore reality to these obvious facts. Two other systems were put forward with the same object by Empedocles and Anaxagoras. They had just as much, and just as little, claim to have proved any scientific truth; and in some respects they were more plausible than atomism.

Atomism never advanced an inch beyond the point to which it was carried by Epicurus. It could not advance until it was revived two thousand years later by modern science, armed with the microscope and a habit of testing its hypothesis by experiment. Atomism then turned out to be a more useful hypothesis than its rivals, though within living memory it has been transformed out of all recognition. But its success in recent times is no warrant for exalting ancient atomism as if it had been established scientific truth, or for calling it (as Mr Farrington does) 'the most assured result of Greek speculation' and 'the triumphant solution' of the problem of the constitution of the universe.[1] Nor is it fair to say that it was rejected by idealists like Plato for motives of self-interest or class interest. Plato incorporated a revised form of atomism in his own account of the constitution of matter. But it seemed to him that a theory which reduced all reality to little bits of dead, impenetrable body, moving chaotically in a void, could not account for an ordered universe or for the phenomena of life, including our own minds with their thoughts and feelings. And, whatever materialists may have believed a century ago, no one, I suppose, now holds that all these phenomena can be satisfactorily explained in terms of an unlimited number of billiard-balls, banging about and colliding in empty space.

(2) In the second place, we come to the suggestion that Ionian philosophy was 'useful to humanity', as providing a sound materialistic basis for the application of science to the production of material goods, and so contributing to human progress, as conceived by those who identify progress with an increase of wealth and power. This tendency, we are told, is symbolised by the Prometheus of Aeschylus, the friend of man and inventor of the arts. Prometheus' famous speech is said to expand the theme that his philanthropy 'is identical with the creation of applied science'.[2] Moreover, his ally, the hundred-headed Typho, symbolises 'popular revolt' against the established order.[3] When Aeschylus disapproves of Prometheus' unreasonable rashness and obstinacy, and speaks of Typho as 'hissing forth terror from his horrid jaws', he means that there is danger in the association of 'the eager humanity of the enlightenment' with 'the many-headed people'. On the other side, Zeus is to represent the blind, repressive violence of the oligarchic reactionaries, who had been advised by Theognis to 'trample on the many-headed populace'. Reconciliation can be effected only when 'reform becomes wise and patient and authority becomes instructed and humane'.[4]

This political or social interpretation of the *Prometheus* attributes

[1] Farrington, p. 122. [2] Ibid. p. 68.
[3] Ibid. p. 69. [4] Ibid. pp. 83 f.

to the enlightened philosophy of Ionia two characteristics which I wish to keep distinct. First, it alleges that this philosophy was philanthropic, as pointing the way to material progress; and secondly, that it was a popular philosophy, frowned upon by the ruling class as subversive of the established order.

First, then, was the Ionian philosophy progressive, in the sense of promising to contribute, as applied science, to increased material wealth and power over natural forces? I venture to assert that no spectator, listening to Prometheus' recital of the arts bestowed on man to alleviate his miserable condition, could possibly have associated those arts with the atomic theory or with any other Ionian system. Prometheus taught man to build houses, to count and write, to construct a farmer's calendar, to domesticate animals, build ships, cure diseases with herbs, practise divination, and work in metals. All these arts had, of course, existed for centuries before the Ionians began to describe the origin of the cosmos and to assert that everything was made of water, or air, or atoms, or the four elements. It could not occur to anyone that these speculations had any bearing whatever on possible improvements in the means of production. The belief that bodies consist of atoms or homoeomeries could not help anyone to invent more efficient types of plough or loom. Accordingly, even if Prometheus stands for the restless intellect, driven by necessity to struggle out of savagery into civilisation, there was nothing to connect such material progress with Ionian physics, no question of any philanthropic application of science to human welfare.[1]

Of all the arts enumerated by Prometheus, the one with most pretention to be scientific was medicine; and medicine certainly was philanthropic, since it had always aimed at alleviating human suffering. But medicine had an independent root in the practical treatment of individual cases, ages before it came to develope anything we should call scientific theory or procedure. When it did approach that stage, notably in the Hippocratic School, its characteristic reaction to Ionian physics was a vigorous protest against the intrusion of philosophic dogmas into its own field.

[1] Much the same view of Prometheus appears in Thomson's *Aeschylus and Athens*, pp. 327 f.

The treatise *On Ancient Medicine* insists that the medical art is of great antiquity, and has always had its own secure foundation in the observation of individual patients and in accumulated experience of verifiable fact. The Ionian speculations are denounced as dogmatic assumptions, not based on experience and worse than useless for the philanthropic purposes of the physician. This conflict in aim and method warns us that the philanthropic character of medicine cannot be extended to Ionian physics, as Mr Farrington would have it. From the fact that doctors relieve suffering we cannot argue that the philosophers were bent upon applying science to improve material conditions. It is quite certain that they were not; and the anecdotes current about them show that, in the popular view, they were unpractical head-in-air theorists, who absurdly neglected even their own economic interests.

Finally, it is not easy to see why the existing holders of wealth and power, symbolised by Zeus, should have objected to their advantages being extended by applied science. The modern capitalist does not persecute natural science; he is eager to spend vast sums on industrial research. Epicurus, on the other hand, regarded the pursuit of wealth as a misuse of human energy, no less disastrous than the pursuit of power. He had no wish to control, or to exploit, the forces of Nature; for any accession of power and wealth would have upset that peace of mind which he found in the simplest possible manner of life. If the happiness you desire can best be obtained by living on bread and water in a home-spun shirt, the spectacle of steam agitating the lid of a boiling kettle will not impel you to invent the steam-engine, the power-loom, and the tractor. Epicurus would have felt much more sympathy with Mr Gandhi than (let us say) with Lord Nuffield.

(3) But let us for the moment waive this objection and entertain the view that Prometheus symbolises the 'Ionian enlightenment' in general, allowing this phrase to embrace the natural philosophers, the philanthropic physicians, and the sophistic movement. In opposition to all this, Zeus is to represent the reactionary oligarchs, the rich, who (we are told) were really the ruling class even in the heyday of Athenian democracy. Aeschylus (says Mr

Farrington) saw the problem of government 'in terms of his own day, the brutal *ignorance* of the reaction with its ministers Might and Violence, the eager humanity of the enlightenment and the danger of its association with the many-headed people'. His solution was that 'reform [Prometheus and Typho] should become wise and patient, and authority [Zeus] should become *instructed* and humane'.[1]

What does this solution mean in more concrete terms? It must mean that the ignorant upper class needed to be instructed in the teachings of the philosophers, doctors, sophists, and initiated into the enlightened rationalism which was encouraging the many-headed workers and peasants of Attica to revolt against the established order. Here we come to the third point in Mr Farrington's theory which I wish to challenge. He describes what he calls 'the Ionian renaissance' as 'in a very real sense a *popular* movement of enlightenment'.[1] In proof of its popular character, he quotes a medical treatise, of the age of the sophists in the late fifth century, which mentions a considerable public interest in discussions of the conflict between philosophy and medicine. At the same time Euripides was introducing the theories of his friend Anaxagoras to his 'somewhat backward fellow-citizens' in the theatre. Earlier still Xenophanes had recited his poems in many Greek cities. On these grounds the Ionian philosophers are enlisted under the banner of Prometheus on the side of the many-headed people in the class-war; and in the fourth century Plato is cast for the role of the ignorant and reactionary Zeus.

This picture of Ionian enlightenment as a popular movement, associated with the emancipation of the poor and oppressed, seems hard to reconcile with the evidence of fifth-century writers. The *Clouds* of Aristophanes does not suggest that the atheistical rationalism there taught by Socrates was familiar and congenial to the peasantry, as represented by Strepsiades; nor do we hear that it was any more familiar in the workshops of the urban craftsmen. The friends of Anaxagoras were to be found in the circle of Pericles and Aspasia; and, even if Euripides' mother was really a greengrocer, the poet himself was not a typical proletarian.

[1] Pp. 84, 33. [The italics in these quotations are Cornford's.—W.K.C.G.]

Prometheus is called by Mr Thomson 'the patron-saint of the proletariat', and the proletariat of antiquity were, he tells us, the slave population. But it was not an audience of slaves, or of workers and peasants, that met at the house of the wealthy Callias to hear the great sophists, Protagoras, Hippias, and Prodicus. The sophists lectured to young men of the upper class who had leisure to attend and were rich enough to pay their fees. It was Plato's misfortune to be born into that class; but if, like the Zeus of Aeschylus, he was an ignorant reactionary, who (says Mr Farrington) 'relentlessly opposed the Ionian scientific tradition and the spread of popular enlightenment',[1] it was not because he failed to become instructed and humane by joining a workers' educational association. And when we come to Epicurus, the last flower of Ionian enlightenment, is there a single line in his writings, or in Lucretius, which betrays the smallest concern for the social welfare either of the poorer citizens or of the slave proletariat? The Memmius addressed by Lucretius was probably a rather disreputable aristocrat; and the poet speaks of the atomic theory, not as a widespread popular doctrine, but as so obscure and repellent that all the honey of the Muse is required to sweeten the draught of wormwood from which 'the multitude shrink back in dismay'.[2]

Here I must end the review of this side of Mr Farrington's argument, which I hope I have not misrepresented. I conclude that his attempt to picture the Ionian philosophy of nature as genuinely scientific in the modern sense, as a philanthropic impulse towards material progress, and as the outcome of a popular movement, is dictated by a conviction that the facts must fit the frame of a materialist interpretation of all history, which is the characteristic product of the early nineteenth century.

The rest of my time must be given to offering some apology for that reactionary oligarch, Plato. Mr Farrington's main thesis is that, in ancient society, the problem for the oligarch was: how

[1] P. 130.

[2] Lucr. iv. 8 ff. I cannot agree with Mr Farrington's interpretation of these last words as meaning that Lucretius 'clearly thinks that, if he can succeed in interesting Memmius, he may succeed in reaching a wider audience too, the general mass of the people, whom the poem is meant to serve' (p. 184).

to 'disseminate such ideas as would make the unjust distribution of the rewards and toils of life seem a necessary part of the eternal constitution of things, and to suppress such ideas as might lead to criticism of this view of the universe'.[1] The operation of this political principle was, he maintains, a major cause of the degeneration of science from Anaximander to the final triumph of Christianity.

In this campaign of the rich to keep the poor in their places by suppressing truth and disseminating superstition, the sinister part assigned to Plato is succinctly described by Mr Thomson. He tells us that, after the Peloponnesian War, Athenian thought was sharply divided between the few who had an interest in maintaining the city-state, and those who had not. (The implication that the abolition of the city-state would have entailed the abolition of social inequalities, including slavery, is hard to justify in the light of history.) 'The idealists', he writes, 'clung to their faith in the city-state at the cost of accepting social inequalities which were becoming less and less compatible with honest thinking.... Plato made slavery the basis of his ideal state, modelled on the parasitic communism of backward Spartan landowners, and, true to his model, passed imaginary laws narrowly restricting the activities of painters and poets, in whose creative imagination and fertile sense of human possibilities he recognised a danger to the established order; while, for the further security of his ruling class, he drew up a fantastic system of education designed to poison the minds of the people by dissemination of calculated lies.'[2]

Mr Thomson has here combined two different accusations against Plato. One is that he proposed to keep the structure of the city-state, and did not foresee that it was 'entering on its last phase'. This is true; and Aristotle was no wiser. But what contemporary of Plato displayed more foresight? The materialist whom Mr Thomson and Mr Farrington hold up in contrast, is Epicurus, who was born six or seven years after Plato's death, and was a boy when Alexander's conquests transformed the political scene and destroyed the independence of the city-states.

[1] P. 27. [2] *Aeschylus and Athens*, p. 368.

The second accusation rests on quite other grounds. The city-state was a frame within which any type of constitution could subsist: a despotism, an oligarchy, or a democracy. Any Greek citizen of Plato's day, rich or poor, would have been completely puzzled, if he had been told that he had no interest in maintaining the structure of the city-state. The democrat, in particular, would have replied: 'Do you really think that an oriental despotism, where all men but one are slaves, is a higher and happier type of society? Or would you reduce us to the level of those savages with all their queer customs described by Herodotus?' When Mr Thomson speaks of 'the few who had an interest in maintaining the city-state', he is suggesting that Plato, being himself well-to-do, 'sought to stabilise society on the basis of the exclusive domination of a leisured class', like the Spartan landowners, that is, to reduce all city-states to oligarchies or plutocracies (as Xenophon calls them), ruled by the few whose interest it was to maintain, *not* the framework of the city-state, but a plutocratic form of government. Mr Farrington, in the same strain, calls Plato's system the philosophy of an oligarch. 'It was', he writes, 'to banish for ever the possibility of popular revolts and to establish a class-divided society on a secure basis that he sought to call in the aid of the governmental lie, and so to stamp it upon the soul of the people that they should be for ever incapable of questioning its truth.'[1]

Even Mr Crossman, in his lively work *Plato Today*, describes the ideal state as 'not a democracy of rational equals, but an aristocracy in which a hereditary caste of cultured gentlemen care with paternal solicitude for the toiling masses'.[2] And he represents Plato as capable of admiring the use of propaganda or 'noble lies' in modern totalitarian states.

May I now, by way of contrast, briefly recall what Plato did in fact propose? In the *Republic* his fundamental thesis is that the inborn disposition which can develop the highest qualities of intellect and character required to make a good ruler, is very rarely found and very easily corrupted. The human race will not see the end of trouble until society is effectively controlled by the

[1] P. 94 (cf. p. 119).　　　　[2] *Plato Today*, p. 132.

few men and women in whom those qualities have been developed to the full by an arduous moral and intellectual training and by experience in practical life. Plato was an oligarch and an aristocrat in the sense that he thought mankind can be well governed only by a few, and those few the wisest and best. He also believed that the capacities required are normally inherited, but may appear in any stratum of society. They can be discovered and brought to the front only as they emerge in childhood and youth. Accordingly, all children of all the citizens in the ideal state are to receive the same elementary education, during which their behaviour, under tests of every sort, will be carefully watched. The most promising will be sifted out, without any regard to their parentage, and given a higher university education in the exact sciences and moral philosophy, lasting for fifteen years. At every stage a further selection will be made. After another fifteen years of practical experience in subordinate posts, the small company of men and women, who have come through every test of intellect and character, will form the supreme council of state. Their qualification to rule is the highest wisdom man can attain—an understanding of the order of the universe and of the true values of all the things that men desire. They will know what really makes life worth living, and that you cannot make a state or an individual happy by making them richer or more powerful than their neighbours. All these rulers and the subordinate guardians are forbidden to own money, houses, or land. They live in monastic austerity, on a bare subsistence provided by the third order, the Producers, who have not qualified for the higher education. This order includes, not merely what Mr Crossman calls 'the toiling masses' and the Marxians call 'the workers', but all owners of property, business men, merchants, shopkeepers, craftsmen, farmers. These will continue to live a normal family life. All the wealth of the city is in their hands; but no one is to be either rich or poor, because any sharp distinction of riches and poverty would entail the class-war and destroy the unity of the commonwealth. But this third order is restricted to its useful and necessary economic functions, and is denied any part in politics. The Producers, in return for the wages they pay to the Guardians, will receive good government at the hands of those who are wiser than they, and who have proved, both by temperament and by training, superior alike to the profit-making and pleasure-loving motives, and to all ambition for worldly power.

In the review of degenerate types of constitution in Book VIII the Spartan timocracy is condemned as corrupted by secret avarice; and oligarchy or plutocracy is ranked still lower as a constitution fraught with many evils.

Such being Plato's proposals, it seems unfair to assert that what he 'really' wanted was to perpetuate the exclusive domination of a leisured class of property-owners or to substitute for Athenian democracy 'an aristocracy in which a hereditary caste of cultured gentlemen care with paternal solicitude for the toiling masses'. If such had been his intention, he would have framed a constitution like the English squirearchy of the eighteenth century, instead of proposing a resolution which would have given Squire Western an apoplectic fit.

Mr Thomson has added the still graver charge, that Plato, 'for the further security of his ruling class, drew up a fantastic system of education designed to poison the minds of the people by dissemination of calculated lies'.[1] Mr Crossman's language is milder (he is not a Marxian); but he describes the elementary education provided for all citizens as consisting of 'propaganda', which Plato called the 'noble lie', 'the technique of controlling the behaviour of the stupid majority'. 'Philosophy and reason are poison to the masses', who 'need not truth, but a convenient falsehood', and 'must be forbidden to eat of the tree of the knowledge of good and evil—for their own sakes'.[2]

Between Mr Thomson and Mr Crossman, the unfortunate Plato could hardly have escaped the charge of being a poisoner. Mr Crossman says he believed reason and philosophy to be poison to the masses; yet, when he offered them propaganda instead, Mr Thomson tells us he was poisoning their minds with calculated lies. His motives too seem, at first sight, somewhat confused. According to Mr Crossman, the masses were denied access to truth *for their own sakes*: it was useless to explain the truth to the

[1] *Aeschylus and Athens*, p. 368.   [2] *Plato Today*, pp. 130-1.

stupid majority. But Mr Thomson insinuates that Plato's purpose was to perpetuate the exclusive domination of his own class. Perhaps the inconsistency was due to 'dishonest thinking'. At the best, we might hope that the pretence of keeping the masses in ignorance for their own good concealed from Plato himself, as well as from others, his secret desire to secure the pre-eminence of the cultured squire. But neither of our critics would let him off with this rather shabby excuse. The propaganda forming the substance of elementary education is, we are told, deliberate and calculated lying.

Once more, let us turn from these accusations to the text of the *Republic*. The education there outlined, so far from being 'fantastic', is (as Plato remarks) simply the traditional Athenian education in poetry and music, with the addition of a university course in pure mathematics and the discussion of moral concepts. It laid down the basic pattern which has persisted through the Middle Ages into our own classical schools and universities. In the elementary stage, the modifications proposed by Plato consist chiefly in the expurgation of the myths from which the Greek child derived his notions of divine and heroic character. The fictions of the poets are denounced, not merely as politically inexpedient, but as false. In particular the gods ought to be represented as entirely good and truthful—incapable of causing any evil or of deluding mankind. More than any other Greek writer, Plato insists on the supreme value, not only of knowing the truth, but of truthfulness. 'A love of truth and a hatred of falsehood that will not tolerate untruth in any form' is declared to be the masterpassion of the philosophic rulers, on which all their other qualifications depend.[1] It seems strange that, in the all-important sphere of education, their business should be to disseminate calculated lies, in order to secure their own social predominance. But if that was not their business, how (we may be asked) could Plato use the expression 'noble lie', which will be found in some translations of a single passage in the *Republic*? It occurs nowhere else.

The answer is that 'noble lie' is simply a mistranslation of the

[1] *Rep.* 475, 485, 490.

phrase γενναῖόν τι ἓν ψευδομένους.[1] Γενναῖον means 'noble' only
in the sense in which we might speak of a 'noble sirloin of beef':
the word, and its equivalent οὐκ ἀγεννής, are frequently used by
Plato for anything that is on a grand scale, or impressive, or
spirited. Much more important is the plain fact that ψεῦδος cannot, in this context, mean a 'lie', if a lie is a false statement made
with intent to deceive. ψεῦδος has a wide range of meaning; it
can cover any statement which is not a literal prosaic statement of
fact. Myth, poetry, fable, romance are all ψεῦδος, *fiction*. Davies
and Vaughan's rendering of γενναῖόν τι ἓν ψευδομένους by 'a single
spirited fiction' is pretty close to Plato's meaning. The expression
is used to introduce an allegorical myth, which the founders of
the ideal state may hope to incorporate in its traditions, so that in
time it will be accepted by all the citizens, including the rulers
themselves. The first lesson this myth conveys is that the citizens
must think of their native land as a mother to be defended from
all attack, and of their fellow-citizens as brothers born of the same
soil. Secondly, the symbolism of Hesiod's races of Gold, Silver,
and Iron, is employed to illustrate the fundamental thesis, that men
are not all born with the same natural capacities. Society, therefore, should be so stratified that the wisest—in whatever stratum
they may be born—shall rise to the top as rulers, and the rest find
their level in lower strata, performing, for the good of the whole,
the useful functions of which they prove capable.

Such is the so-called 'noble lie', denounced by our Marxian
friends as poisonous propaganda. But I submit that a philosopher
who offers for universal acceptance a myth or legend embodying,
in allegorical imagery, what he holds to be the most important
of political truths, is not poisoning anyone's mind with a calculated
lie. Further, it is plainly false to accuse Plato of designing this
fiction in order to perpetuate the domination of his own class—
a 'hereditary aristocracy of cultured gentlemen'—and to keep the
'toiling masses' in permanent subjection. For this very allegory
declares that, if the rulers find a child of their own whose metal
is alloyed with iron or brass, 'they must, without the least pity,
assign him the station proper to his nature, and thrust him out

[1] *Rep.* 414 B.

among the craftsmen and farmers. If, on the contrary, these classes produce a child with gold or silver in his composition, they will promote him, according to his value, to be a Guardian.'[1]

It is true that, once the individual's proper level has been determined, Plato said that he must stay on that level; and he may have been rash in assuming that the several types of disposition—the lovers of wealth, the lovers of power, and the lovers of truth—could be sorted out in their early years. This may be impracticable, like some other features of the ideal state. It may be that the human race is condemned never to see the end of trouble, because it will never find a way to prevent the men who worship power and wealth from gripping the levers of the political machine. Plato himself had no sanguine hope of success; and any materialist is at liberty to think him a fool for saying that an ideal is none the worse for not being capable of realisation.

If our critics will abandon the term 'noble lie', and use the milder word 'propaganda', we may remind them that propaganda is not necessarily false; and that no wholehearted admirer of any totalitarian régime is entitled to object to propaganda in elementary education. It is only from the standpoint of Liberalism that Plato's position is assailable. Like the Catholic Church, he did not believe that truth will have the best chance of making its way, if an un-restricted field is left open to free thought and free speech. In its extreme form this Liberal principle has never, I suppose, been adopted by any human society. Civilised man, like the savage, has always been at pains to mould the beliefs and habits of children into some conformity with the traditional religion and morals of the group. The points at issue between the Liberal on the one hand and the authoritarian on the other are: the extent to which this socialising process should be carried, and the sort of truth that may legitimately be inculcated by authority. Is it the provisional truths of natural science and human history; or an absolute revealed truth, like Catholic Christianity; or a doctrine of political expediency, as in Nazi Germany or Russia?

Plato's attitude to these questions is too authoritarian for the taste of an English Liberal. The Hellenic world, in his time, was

[1] *Rep.* 415 B. Promotion is mentioned again at 423 C.

not indeed in possession of a revealed religion; but he thought that absolute truth might be discoverable in the realm of morals as well as in the field of mathematical science. If so, it could be discovered by the exercise of intuitive reason, a faculty which he sometimes declares to be present in every human soul.[1] When it had been discovered it would provide a faith that might be pro-pagated without reproach. But strait is the gate and narrow the way that leads to wisdom. Ultimate truth was not (as Mr Cross-man suggests) a sort of trade secret of the 'ruling class', arbitrarily withheld from the stupid majority because it would poison them. Anyone may have access to it, in the same sense that it is now open to anyone to grasp the theory of relativity. But the multitude can never be philosophers. They must accept moral truth on trust from those who know. It will be conveyed to them in the imaginative symbolism of poetry and myth. If this is to be called propaganda, we must equally apply that term to the parables in which Christ taught the fishermen of Galilee. Plato constantly calls it 'true belief'. He nowhere speaks of it as belief which, although false, will be useful to the ruling class.

Moral truth was, to Plato's mind, inseparable from religious truth. Mr Farrington gallantly upholds the religion of Epicurus in contrast with the religion of Plato. When we compare the two, we find that neither philosopher proposed to interfere with the traditional state-cults, to which they both conformed. Conformity, of course, did not imply belief in the mythical accounts of the gods. Both attempted to reform popular conceptions of the anthropomorphic gods in accordance with the ethical principles they respectively maintained. Yet Plato is accused of a 'reactionary reimposition of a mass of traditional cults' and of recommending 'the maintenance of all the traditional beliefs', knowing them to be false; whereas Epicurus is praised for accepting 'the religion of the people' and for reforming the 'popular theology' of the average man.[2] An impartial critic (if there were such a person) might wonder how the average man could be expected to feel any religious devotion towards gods who were (like Epicurus himself) egoistic hedonists, as indifferent to human concerns as

[1] *Rep.* 518. [2] Pp. 101, 155.

Epicurus was to all that went on outside his garden and the circle of his friends. The Marxist does not defend the Epicurean religion as true, or as having any sound scientific foundation; but he views with equanimity the social consequences of assuring the wicked man that, if he pursues his own personal pleasure, he has nothing to fear from gods who do exist but are as selfish as himself. The Platonists were not alone in preferring a type of religion which taught that the gods were good and cared for man, and that wickedness which escaped punishment here would be punished after death. The doctrine of immortality and a better lot for the initiate was not a feature of those state-cults, which are alleged to have been kept up by the aristocracy for the sake of their class interests. It belonged to the mysteries, and in particular to the Orphic mysteries. In these, as at Eleusis, distinctions of nationality and class, even the distinction of freeman and slave, were ignored. Orphism really was a popular movement, just because it transcended these distinctions and, like Christianity, held out hope to the poor and oppressed. It was closely related to Pythagoreanism, and Plato's doctrine of immortality was deeply influenced by both. Mr Farrington never mentions Orphism at all. No reader of his book could guess that such a popular religious movement had ever existed. It would not fit into his picture of the oligarch Plato, disseminating 'such ideas as would make the unjust distribution of the rewards and toils of life seem a necessary part of the eternal constitution of things'. This can only mean that the author of the *Republic* taught immortality and the redress of earthly injustice after death, because he wished to perpetuate injustice in this life.

Epicurus, it is true, abolished the terrors of hell; but he also abolished the joys of heaven. Mr Farrington speaks of his doctrine, that the personality is annihilated at the moment of death, as conveying 'a healing balm to all that needed it'.[1] I wonder how many readers have found a healing balm in the third book of Lucretius. I do not know how common the horror of death may be among normal people; but, where it exists, is it not often the prospect of extinction that horrifies them? If so, the fear of death,

[1] P. 125.

which Epicurus claimed to have banished, is actually increased by the denial of immortality. Is it Plato's fault that Western humanity has, on the whole, rejected the Epicurean consolation?

In this short review I have had to leave many arguments unanswered. Let me repeat, in conclusion, that I am not denying that the economic interpretation of history has thrown some light on religious and philosophical speculation in its broad outline. But the narrower the field you take, and the closer you come to individual prophets and thinkers, the less possible it becomes to correlate their doctrines with economic motives or changes in the production of material goods. In the sixth, fifth and fourth centuries we are confronted with a constellation of great men without parallel in the world's history. It is, I believe, good Marxian doctrine that great personalities are accidents, which may temporarily disturb the march of historic events, as an earthquake may deflect a stream without wholly changing its main course. The philosophers' systems and the poets' visions of life are the creations of highly individualised and exceptional minds. I suggest that they should be regarded rather as a chapter of accidents than as secondary reflections of a continuous flow of social or economic change. How else can we account for the fact that philosophers and poets belonging to the same social class, in societies of the same type, with the same modes of production and exchange, contradict one another and hold views as widely divergent as they could possibly be?

APPENDIX

A list of Cornford's publications on classical subjects
(excluding reviews)

A. BOOKS

Thucydides Mythistoricus (Arnold, 1907).

From Religion to Philosophy (Arnold, 1912).

The Origin of Attic Comedy (Arnold, 1914, reprinted by Cambridge, 1934).

Greek Religious Thought (Dent's 'Library of Greek Thought', 1914).

The Laws of Motion in Ancient Thought (Inaugural Lecture, Cambridge, 1931).

Before and After Socrates (Cambridge, 1932).

Aristotle's 'Physics' (with P. H. Wicksteed, Loeb Classical Library, 2 vols. 1929 and 1934).

Plato's Theory of Knowledge (Kegan Paul, 1935).

Plato's Cosmology (Kegan Paul, 1937).

Plato and Parmenides (Kegan Paul, 1939).

Plato's 'Republic' (translated with introduction and notes, Oxford, 1941).

B. CONTRIBUTIONS TO BOOKS

'The Origin of the Olympic Games' (in J. E. Harrison, *Themis*, Cambridge, 1912, 2nd ed. 1927).

'The *Aparchai* and the Eleusinian Mysteries' (in *Essays and Studies presented to William Ridgeway*, Cambridge, 1913).

'Memoir of A. W. Verrall' (in Verrall, *Collected Literary Essays*, ed. Bayfield and Duff, Cambridge, 1913).

'Mystery-Religions and Presocratic Philosophy' (in *Cambridge Ancient History*, vol. IV, 1926).

'The Athenian Philosophical Schools' (in *Cambridge Ancient History*, vol. VI, 1927).

'The Invention of Space' (in *Essays presented to Gilbert Murray*, Allen and Unwin, 1936).

'Greek Natural Philosophy and Modern Science' (in *Background to Modern Science*, Cambridge, 1938).

C. CONTRIBUTIONS TO PERIODICALS

Classical Review
  'Plato and Orpheus' (XVII, 1903).
  'Elpis and Eros' (XXI, 1907).
  'Hermes-Nous and Pan-Logos' (XXVI, 1912).
  'The so-called Kommos in Greek Tragedy' (XXVII, 1913).
  'The Idea of Immortality' (XXXVII, 1923).
  'Note on Aeschylus, *Eumenides* 945' (XXXVIII, 1924).
  'Note on Plato, *Theaetetus* 209 D' (XLIV, 1930).
  'Note on [Plato,] *Eryxias* 393 B' (XLVI, 1932).
  'A New Fragment of Parmenides' (XLIX, 1935).
  'Notes on the *Oresteia*' (LIII, 1939).
Classical Quarterly
  'Note on Plato, *Phaedo* 105 A' (III, 1909).
  'Hermes, Pan, Logos' (III, 1909).
  'Psychology and Social Structure in the *Republic* of Plato' (VI, 1912).
  'Mysticism and Science in the Pythagorean Tradition' (XVI and XVII, 1922 and 1923).
  'Anaxagoras' Theory of Matter' (XXIV, 1930).
  'Aristotle, *Physics* 250 A 9–19 and 266 A 12–24' (XXVI, 1932).
  'Parmenides' Two Ways' (XXVII, 1933).
  'Innumerable Worlds in Presocratic Philosophy' (XXVIII, 1934).
  'Aristotle, *De caelo* 288 A 2–9' (XXXIII, 1939).
Journal of Hellenic Studies
  'Was the Ionian Philosophy Scientific?' (LXII, 1942).
Greece and Rome
  'Plato's Commonwealth' (IV, 1935).
Mind
  'Mathematics and Dialectic in Plato, *Republic* VI and VII' (XLI, N.S. 1932).
  'The "Polytheism" of Plato: an Apology' (XLVII, N.S. 1938).
Hibbert Journal
  'The Division of the Soul' (XXVIII, 1930).
New Adelphi
  'Psychology and the Drama' (I, 1927; originally printed as 'The Origin of the Drama' in Transactions of *New Ideals in Education*, 1922).
Newnham College Letter
  'Memoir of Jane Ellen Harrison' (1929).